John Sentamu's Hope Stories

TO

John & Muriel,

Best wishes,

JSentamu

John Sentamu's Hope Stories

20 True Stories of Faith Changing Lives Today

Presented by the Archbishop of York, Dr John Sentamu

Stories written by
Carmel Thomason

DARTON · LONGMAN + TODD

First published in 2014 by
Darton, Longman and Todd Ltd
1 Spencer Court
140 – 142 Wandsworth High Street
London SW18 4JJ

ISBN: 978-0-232-53109-1

A catalogue record for this book is available from the British Library.

Phototypeset by Kerrypress Ltd, Luton, Beds
Printed and bound in Great Britain by Bell & Bain, Glasgow

Contents

1 'Power in saying how you feel'

Jasvinder Sanghera

'So God created humankind in his image, in the image of God he created them; male and female he created them' (Genesis 1:27).

'For this reason a man leaves his father and mother and clings to his wife, so that they become one flesh' (Genesis 2:24).

'Be subject to one another out of reverence for Christ' (Ephesians 5:21).

John Sentamu writes:

God created man and woman for partnership, mutual comfort and joy. And, for Christians, marriage is exemplified by Jesus Christ's loving and nurturing relationship with his Church.

Jasvinder's disturbing story reveals a picture of marriage that is far removed from this ideal. She endures shame and disgrace, and painful alienation from her family before being lifted up and restored to a life in which she can rediscover the honour and dignity given to human beings by God in his creation.

Through years of perseverance and hope, God gave her strength, not only to forgive those who had rejected her, but to reach out with help to others who were suffering in the same way.

✝

Jasvinder Sanghera's story:

I first learned I was promised to be married when I came home from school and my mother showed me a photograph of a man I didn't know and told me he was to be my husband. I was fourteen years old and my parents had agreed this marriage six years earlier.

I hadn't been expecting it, but I understood something of what my mother was telling me because I'd watched the same thing happen to my older sisters. At age fifteen my sisters went to India and came back as someone's wife. That was how it was in our community, but on returning my sisters didn't seem happy, and I didn't want that life for myself. I wanted to do my exams and go to college. I didn't want to marry a stranger and I told my parents so.

A year later the wedding preparations began. A wedding dress was purchased and people started to come to our house to visit the bride-to-be, who was me. That was when I really protested. 'I'm not marrying a stranger,' I insisted, 'I want to finish school.'

I didn't go back to school after that. My parents shut me in a room with a padlock on the outside of the door and told me that I couldn't leave until I agreed to the marriage. I was kept prisoner by my parents for what seemed like weeks, but it was probably in reality about ten days. Even when I attempted suicide it didn't make any difference to my situation. No one sought medical attention for me, my parents just walked me up and down, giving me lots of coffee to drink. In addition to the physical abuse, my mother used a lot of emotional blackmail to try to sway me to her way of thinking. She told me that if I didn't marry this man, then the shame would cause my father to have a heart attack and it would be my fault. In the end I agreed to the marriage, but it was purely as a plan to escape. Whatever happened, I was determined that I wouldn't marry this stranger.

My mother didn't view the man as a stranger. Her and my father's union had been a similar arrangement when she was a teenager. My father came to the UK in the late 1950s from a very rural village in the Punjab of India, and my mother joined him much later. Our household operated on a system of honour, and one way of bringing dishonour onto the family was to question a marriage. Speaking outside of the family was also a cause of shame, so we never spoke about what was happening and the abuse remained hidden for years.

I don't know why I was the daughter to question what was happening. Perhaps it was because since I was small I was always told that I was different. I was the only one of my parents' eight children to be born in a hospital, I was born upside down, and I have a mole on my right cheek that my family constantly tried to rub off. Now, in planning to escape, I was doing something more different than any of my community could imagine.

Once I'd agreed to the marriage, I was allowed to move around the house, and while I couldn't go back to school I was allowed to visit a friend from an Asian family who lived nearby. I begged her brother to help me, and one day I left my parents a note and we ran away together to Newcastle-upon-Tyne, sleeping in parks and washing in public conveniences. My parents reported me missing to the police, but thankfully when an officer caught up with me he believed my story. I explained that I was being forced to marry against my will and the policeman agreed that he wouldn't tell my parents where I was, so long as I made a call to let them know I was safe.

My mother answered the phone. At the time I thought that by running away, my parents would understand just how upset I was at the idea of this marriage and would begin to see my side. I explained how much I was missing everyone and how I wanted to come home, but I didn't want to marry this stranger.

My mother said: 'You either come home and marry who we say or from this day forward you are dead in our eyes.' It took a long time for those words to sink in. I thought that she was just angry, but she reinforced it by adding, 'You have shamed and dishonoured the family.' As if that wasn't enough, my mother told me that I'd never amount to anything, that I'd be rolling around the streets forever, I'd become a prostitute and I'd give birth to a daughter who would do the same to me as I'd done to her – then I'd know how it feels.

I heard her words, but part of me still believed that in time my family would come round to my way of thinking. Regardless of the abuse that was happening, this was still my family, the people I had grown up with, who I loved dearly, and I kept on hoping that one day they would accept me back into their lives. I made phone calls home for three years, but the abuse and rejection was always the same. My only solace came when two of my sisters began to talk to me in secret.

When I was 18 years old I visited Whitley Bay and saw the sea for the first time. I remember thinking, 'Wow, if this is on the planet, what else is there?' Standing on the beach gave me a great sense of hope that there was so much more I could do with my life. I'd made my choice and I had to get on with it. So, I set myself up as a market trader, married the boy who had helped me to run away and gave birth to our daughter the following year. Having a child of my own made me realise what it meant to love someone unconditionally. I wished I could have shared that joy with my family, but even knowing they had another grandchild didn't change my parents' view.

I started to visit my sister, Rabina who was a mother now too. I would meet her in secret and she would tell me how unhappy she was in her marriage. I tried to persuade her to leave. 'That's easy for you to say because you don't have to think about honour,' she told me. She was right. I'd already been cast out, so those things weren't at the forefront of my mind anymore. Then, one day a woman came to my market stall and told me I should ring home because something had happened.

My mother answered the phone. 'It's Rabina, she died. She committed suicide. She set herself on fire and she's dead.' I wanted to go to the house, but I was reminded of my position of shame and dishonour. After persistence I was allowed to visit after dark when no one would see me.

After the funeral we were not allowed to speak of Rabina again. I was so angry that the concept of honour was being put before a human life – that it was better for Rabina to take her life than to leave her husband and bring dishonour on the family. All these years I'd carried around this label of being a horrible, mean person who had done terrible things to my family. I began to realise that there was nothing unworthy about me – I was a victim. My anger over-rode the fear I once had, and I decided that I wasn't going to let them treat me like this anymore. I'd done nothing wrong, there was no reason for me to hide, so I moved back to my hometown of Derby.

My mother's health deteriorated rapidly after Rabina's death, although she never spoke of her. When she became terminally ill we had a secret relationship, always on my mother's terms. I wasn't allowed to visit her at the hospice when the rest of the family was there, and would have to visit in the middle of the night. When the nurses told me that her death was imminent, my mother asked me to leave. I refused and the family arrived to see me by her bed. They were all shocked – our dirty little secret was out. 'Just leave it now,' my mother said, and her last words were, 'Rabina, I'm coming to you.'

My mother's death wasn't the end of my family differences. I was still shamed. My marriage broke down; having no family to turn to for support, I was vulnerable to unhealthy relationships and married again in haste. The marriage was unhappy but I stayed because I had nowhere else to go. In my heart I kept telling myself, this is not my life, this can't be my life. I knew that I needed to get a job to enable me to protect my children and bring them up to have a better life, but with no qualifications what could I do? I decided to get back into education and nervously signed up with the local college.

I was 27-years-old before I read a book, but once I started the classes I realised that I could learn, that I did have intelligence, and that I wasn't worthless. In that same year I set up Karma Nirvana, to help other women speak about their experiences of forced marriage. The name means peace and enlightenment, because if you have choices then you can achieve a sense of peace. I didn't think about it as a charity at this time, I just believed that the silence had to be broken. I was teaching keep fit classes and when women would talk to me afterwards about their personal lives I'd tell them about this organisation that could help. When I say organisation, it was just a phone in my front room, but it was something.

I'd always carried a sense that I wasn't clever, but once I passed my A levels I began to gain confidence and went on to study social and cultural studies at university. In my final year my marriage broke down irretrievably while I was pregnant with my son. It wasn't easy, but with the support of two women who became great friends I managed to finish my studies and graduated with a first class honours degree. I was the only one of my family to graduate and I sent my father an invitation to the ceremony, at which I was asked to give the student vote of thanks. He never came. I remember looking out from the stage and seeing my three children. It was the first time I'd spoken in front of an audience and as I started talking the script I'd written didn't seem the right thing to say anymore. Instead, I thanked my father and mother, because if it wasn't for them then I wouldn't be standing in Britain being able to be educated. For the first time, I felt no anger towards them. Regardless of what had happened, I felt immensely grateful to my parents for taking the decision to travel all that way and make the UK their home. I started to speak about my personal experience and the words kept coming. When I finished the audience all rose to their feet clapping, and I realised that there is power in simply saying what you think and feel.

I had been angry for so long, but it was time to let all the hurt go. At the same time I decided to let God in too, to learn more about forgiveness and to embrace the good things in my life, like my children, my health and my gift for being able to speak about my experiences and having people who would listen. For a long time doors would close in my face and people didn't want to hear what I had to say because I was clouded by resentment and rejection. I realised that my anger had been holding me back. I stopped grieving the loss of my family and began to put my energy into Karma Nirvana. I believed in it completely. Volunteers would ask me, 'Do victims ever call the helpline?' and I'd reply, 'They will one day, trust me.' It took four years to get our first call, but to date we have assisted 30,000 victims on our helpline, more victims are speaking out, and this year forced marriage became a criminal offence in the UK.

When my father died, unbeknown to me, he made me an executor of his will. I was the only one in the family who had been disowned. I was the only one made to feel unworthy, and yet here was my father entrusting me with his will. After his death I went into his house for the first time. In the corner of his bedroom, my graduation photograph was hanging on the wall. I remember sending it to him, but never knowing if he'd received it because I didn't get a reply. Seeing that photograph framed, in a place where my father would have looked on it every day, gave me a sense that, although he could never tell me when he was alive, my father thought I was a good person.

2 'The Lord has forgiven me'

Jim Race

'God did not send his Son into the world to judge the world, but in order that the world might be saved through him' (John 3:17).

John Sentamu writes:

God sent his only Son Jesus into this world, not to judge or condemn us, but so that we might be saved. We are given the chance to draw closer to God, in the midst of whatever troubles we face. God is always ready to forgive but it can take real courage to trust in that forgiveness and start again with God, Father, Son and Holy Spirit, and with others.

Sometimes we can all fail to miss the point of an exercise. We don't listen properly to the instructions or feel that we know best. We can start off on the wrong foot which sets us back or we set out in entirely the wrong direction and follow the wrong path. Trying to put things right can seem an impossible task, and finding where to start becomes a real challenge.

Working out what is expected of us or what God's plan is for each of us is a lifetime's passion and taking the first step is always the hardest.

Jim's story is about taking his first steps, gaining confidence and trust. In following Jesus Christ, he found love, joy, peace, patience, kindness, generosity, faithfulness, gentleness and self-control. What are you waiting for?

✞

Jim Race's story:

There are many different routes I could take into York. I don't know why this particular Monday morning I chose to walk along High Petergate, because it was slightly out of my way, or why I chose to go back to talk to two men I'd decided were nutcases, but I'm pleased I did.

At the time I was lost in every sense. In the past when everything was going wrong I had always managed to pick myself up and build up what I'd lost, but this time for whatever reason I realised that I didn't have that same verve any more.

Walking along I noticed a cage outside St Michael le Belfrey Church. Well, you couldn't miss it really because inside it were two men dressed in bright orange coveralls. 'Lunatics!' I thought, crossing the road to avoid them. 'York is full of lunatics.'

I carried on walking, telling myself how awful it was that there were so many nutcases on the streets these days, but something inside me was inquisitive. I had to go back and ask what they were doing.

The young men told me their names were Luke and Gav, and they were living in this small cage for a week without any provisions, knowing that the Lord would provide.

'People find themselves trapped in all sorts of situations,' said Luke, 'sometimes through no fault of their own, but we believe that Jesus can bring freedom in any situation.'

This explanation didn't leave me thinking that they were any less strange. 'What happens if nobody brings you any food?' I asked.

'Oh, we know people will,' said Gav.

I couldn't get my head around what they were saying. Someone from the church asked if I'd like a chair and brought me a cup of tea. So, there I was sitting comfortably, drinking my tea and talking to these two chaps who had nothing. When I stood up to leave I thought I'd been there for about 20 minutes. It turned out that I'd been talking to them for two-and-a-half hours. I can't remember what we talked about, I just remember finding it so refreshing that they weren't asking for anything from me.

I didn't have much to give at the time. In the past I'd been a professional sportsman, a successful publican and hotelier, running a chain of six pubs. I didn't recognise that man in myself anymore. I felt old. I'd had a series of heart attacks which had forced me to retire on health grounds. I'd lost my relationship, I'd lost my home, and I was living in a hostel for the homeless. The situation was entirely my fault. I'd been married three times and divorced three times. I'd built businesses and I'd lost businesses. I seemed to have a self-destruct button that I had a habit of pressing when things were going well. It was always when I got to the pinnacle of anything that I'd go into a deep depression, which felt as if someone had thrown a wet blanket on me and I couldn't see anything. I wouldn't wash, I wouldn't take phone calls, I didn't even want to get out of bed. I never wanted to kill myself, but at times like that I wanted to go to sleep and not wake up.

The old saying that you always hurt the ones you love was very true in my case. I'd lash out at my nearest and dearest, anyone who was trying to lift me out of the depression. In the end that kind of behaviour drives people away and it did. Usually something would happen, like the real threat of losing my business, to jolt me out of the depression. It would take me months, maybe a year to build the business back up again. This time, however, I felt I'd pressed the destruct button one time too many, because I couldn't get my life back.

The next day I walked back into York along the same route to see if Gav and Luke were still there. Seeing that they were, I bought them each a pasty and a hot coffee. I couldn't get over the fact that they would just know someone would bring them food and drink, yet every day I took something for them, so I guess they were right. Whether they really needed anything from me didn't matter, because I wanted to give them something. After a couple of days I started to get my own chair out of the church and would sit outside the cage chatting for I don't know how long.

I did that every day for a week, whatever the weather. Indeed the final day was a washout, but I walked into town in the wind and rain nonetheless to be there to see Gav and Luke finally freed. Again we chatted and they invited me to go on an Alpha course at the church. 'Oh, yes, that would be marvellous,' I said, but typical of me at that time, I didn't show up.

A few weeks later I bumped into Gav on the street. 'What happened? You didn't come,' he said.

'No, I was busy,' I replied and went on my way. Within a few minutes I'd bumped into Luke.

'Hey, you never came and we were really looking forward to seeing you,' he said.

Again I made my excuses, 'I couldn't. I've just moved into a new flat and I had to get it sorted because I've got nothing for it.'

It was true that I had just moved into a new flat, because the following week I'd been offered a housing association property. The flat was unfurnished, but I didn't let anyone know that I had nothing to furnish it with. I just wanted a home so I accepted the flat straight away without question. I told myself that because I was moving house I was too busy to go on the Alpha course. It was a convenient excuse. The truth was, I wasn't sure that the course was for me. I thought it would be full of people reading the Bible and praying – that wasn't for me. I didn't understand what it was all about. I had been to church before, but it was such a long time ago. My grandfather was a verger and I always went to Sunday School as a young child. Then between the ages of 11 and 13 I joined the church cricket team. I enjoyed that, but it was a summer sport so once the season had finished, my season at church ended too. When I became too old for the youth cricket team I stopped going to church. There had been no place for Christ in the last 40 years of my life. I didn't pray then and I didn't know how to pray now. If I went along to the Alpha course I was sure that I would make a fool of myself. So, I didn't go and I stayed in the flat, on my own.

'What's your address?' Luke asked. 'We can help you with some furniture. We'll pick you up on Sunday morning and take you to church if you like?'

I didn't know why these lads would be bothered with someone like me but I gave Luke my address and on Sunday morning, just as he said, he arrived. He saw I had nothing in the flat, but he didn't say anything. We drove to church and to my surprise I found that I enjoyed it.

The following week I went back, and then the next, and the next. People at church helped me find furniture for my flat. I started getting involved in church life and became one of the welcoming team on the door. I found the fellowship wonderful. I loved the people, I loved the chance to worship and the chance to ask for forgiveness for everything I'd done. I wanted forgiveness, but I couldn't believe it was possible, not for me, not after everything I'd done in my life and the way I'd treated people. I couldn't believe that the Lord would want me after that.

I told the vicar how I was feeling. 'Just keep faith,' he said. 'The Lord wants you. The Lord forgives everything.'

One Sunday evening, part of the service was about God meeting us where we are and using us as we are. A rush like an electric current ran through my body as I realised, for the first time, that I could be forgiven and that I was forgiven. I felt completely cleansed and it was the most wonderful feeling. I held my arms in the air, singing the hymns at the top of my lungs. This is it, I thought. This is the start of a new life. The Lord has forgiven me and I've forgiven anyone who has ever done anything to me. Everything I've done in the past is written off and I don't need to worry about it. I don't even need to think about it. I can just concentrate on helping as many people as I can.

That Christmas I invited a couple of lads from the hostel to my flat for dinner and asked if one of the chaps on the church welcoming team would like to join us.

'If you're cooking for two, I'd rather us cook for all the homeless if we can,' he said.

'Ok,' I said. 'If you can get the premises, I'll do the cooking.'

We were given permission to use the church hall, but apart from ourselves we had no other resources and we certainly didn't have any money to buy the food we'd need. So, we prayed about it and to our surprise people started donating money.

That first year we fed 68 people on Christmas day and the Christmas after that we fed nearly 200 people. I started getting involved with homeless issues and sitting on a homeless strategy group.

That was four years ago now. There's so much still to do and I sometimes wonder if the Lord has picked the right man, but each time I question if I have the strength to do this the Lord seems to refresh me. A lot of the people I'm helping have problems with alcohol and drugs, but as a publican I was dealing with those issues all the time, so I'm used to it.

I know that, for me, depression is never far away, but I've learned to cope better. I pray and I have great friends in the church who I can ring and talk to at any time. In the past when I started to get depressed, I would slip into a deeper and deeper depression until I reached the point where I couldn't shake it. Now, if I'm starting to feel down I know that there are friends I can call who understand and who will come to meet me. Once we've met and I've talked, the depression doesn't get a grip of me in the same way it used to.

This week I was putting up my Christmas tree. It always makes me smile because I remember that Luke's cell group bought me this tree and lights. 'We're going to get you some Christmas decorations,' Luke said. We all got in the car and parked up in a retail park.

'You don't buy a Christmas tree in an electrical shop', I thought, 'even I know that', but I followed them nevertheless. Then Luke pointed out a fridge freezer. 'Would you like that?' he said.

'Yeah, that would be wonderful,' I said, not thinking he meant, did I want him to buy it for me.

'Right, let's order it and see if we can get it in the car so you can have it today.'

Afterwards, we went out for lunch, while unknown to me someone else from church went food shopping so that my fridge was full when I got home. I couldn't believe anyone would do something like that for me. It was amazing.

I can never thank Luke and Gav enough, but whenever I say that I'm always told, 'Don't thank us, thank the Lord.' I know they mean it and I do thank the Lord. I thank the Lord every day for the hope he has brought into my life.

3 'Taking my heartache away'

Kelly Varley

'May those who sow in tears reap with shouts of joy. Those who go out weeping, bearing the seed for sowing, shall come home with shouts of joy' (Psalm 126:5-6).

John Sentamu writes:

Happiness, which is always dependent on the chances and the changing circumstances, is not the same as joy. Joy is a gift of God's own blessedness which is independent of the chances and circumstances of life. The opposite of joy is not sadness, but fear, anxiety and worry.

The chances and circumstances of life are different for everyone but we should remember that God loves us for who we are, as well as who we might become or have been. We are fearfully and wonderfully made. And in His presence, we find his constant forgiveness and love. His Good News isn't for the chosen few, it is for everyone!

The prophet Isaiah says, *'Fear not for I have redeemed you, I have called you by name, you are mine'* (Isaiah 43:16).

This next chapter is about overcoming fear. Kelly shares her story of accepting the joy which is Christ's free gift to all his friends.

Jesus invites us to receive His Resurrection life and to live it as pure gift. What an awesome invitation of God's love and power. And what a transformation that He brings!

Kelly Varley's story:

It's amazing how much can change in a short time, if you give life a chance. If someone had told me this time last year that I would have regained my confidence, made new friends, be engaged to a wonderful man who I'm completely in love with, and be excited about the future, I'd have laughed. Well, I probably wouldn't have laughed, because I didn't even smile back then. At that time, to have the life I have now seemed impossible. It was beyond anything I could imagine. On some days, I couldn't see myself getting out of bed.

Nothing good ever happened in my life, or that was how it felt. My partner of six years, Richard, was a problem drinker. I was in my early twenties and he was in his forties. You might think because of the age difference that he would be the sensible one, but I had to look after him in a way that I never expected. I never knew what kind of mood he would be in when he arrived home. If he was in a bad mood, I learned to keep out of the way. At other times I'd have to clean him up and sit with him to make sure he was ok – it wasn't nice. It was difficult to cope and we were both on medication just to help us get through the day. There are a lot of things I'm not going to say because they don't need to be said. Despite everything, I did love him. When he wasn't drinking, we had some good times – it wasn't all bad.

I was devastated when Richard died. It was alcohol abuse that killed him in the end. One night after he'd been drinking heavily he vomited blood. I called an ambulance but he was bleeding internally and this time there was nothing anyone could do. I had all of his family around me at the hospital but they couldn't comfort me and I couldn't comfort them. We'd had a health scare with Richard a couple of years earlier. That time he was in hospital for three weeks, and I think it gave him a shock because when he was discharged he did stop drinking for a while and was doing really well. It was hard to watch him start drinking again. Obviously we knew that it wasn't doing him or any of us any good, but we never expected him to die.

I was angry that Richard had left me in this way and I would lie on my bed, punching my pillows until I had no tears left. Life was dark and sad, and I had no hope of it ever changing for me. I felt that I had no one to talk to, no one who would understand. How could they? How could anyone understand when they hadn't been through what I had been through?

I was still grieving for Richard when my uncle died three months later. A few months after that, another uncle passed away. It was too much – I wasn't able to grieve for one person without having to deal with burying someone else close to me.

I recognised the vicar at my uncle's funeral; it was Revd Jimmy Hinton, the same person who had taken Richard's funeral service. After the service Jimmy was shaking hands with everyone outside the church. When it came to my turn, he recognised me too from Richard's funeral and asked how I was. 'I just can't cope with any more,' I said. 'Three bereavements in a year – my head is messed up.' I didn't expect him to say anything, but he gave me his number and said that I could give him a call if I wanted to talk things through.

I didn't do anything for a couple of days, but I kept Jimmy's number. I'm not sure he expected me to respond, but I had a feeling that I could trust him. I knew that he wasn't going to judge me about what happened. Until that point I hadn't felt able to talk to anyone about how I was feeling. Just the thought of talking about what happened made me nervous. What would I say? I didn't have the courage to call Jimmy, so I texted instead – it was the best text message I've ever sent.

I'd kept my emotions bottled up for so long that it was a huge relief to finally open up to someone. I told Jimmy how I felt about Richard dying, how I blamed myself and mulled over and over in my head if there was more I could have done, something that I could have done to make things turn out differently. After our conversation it felt like a weight had been lifted from me. I was tearful, but I was also pleased that I'd done it.

I chatted with Jimmy another couple of times. We talked about the need for me to be around other people, people who would understand and wouldn't judge me in any way. Jimmy was right, I did need to start mixing with people again, but the thought of it was frightening. He said that I could come to church if I liked, but I didn't know anything about it. I worried that everyone would be staring at me, that I'd have to explain what I'd been through and then I'd get the looks, the looks that said more than any words ever could. I just didn't want to do that.

Jimmy left me a book, *No Ordinary Man*, based on Luke's gospel. I only ever went to church for funerals so learning about Jesus was all new to me. The fact that Jesus loved people unconditionally really touched me. Jesus accepted people for who they were, it didn't matter what their faults were, or what they had done, he loved them no matter what.

After reading the book I wanted to go to church because I wanted to find out more about this man, Jesus. I couldn't get over everything he'd done without expecting anything back in return. I didn't have the confidence to go to church on my own, so my cousin, Anthony, who went to another church agreed to come with me. He was a great help, because without him I never would have got through the door and I'm so glad I did.

People came to talk to me and it gave me confidence to think that they accepted me for being me and not for my background or for what I'd been through. They weren't bothered about any of that. It was nice to feel welcome. I joined a fitness class held at the church and started making new friends. Soon I could feel my life changing for the better. It was hard, but I began to accept that Richard was no longer with us, that he wasn't going to walk through the door and that I was never going to see him again. I began to think about the miracle where Jesus heals a blind man and makes him see again. I felt that he was doing something like that in my life. I'd asked Jesus to help me and he was there. He was opening me up and taking my heartache away.

After a while I wanted to get baptised and it was the best thing I've ever done. During the baptism ceremony I got a feeling of warmth. I know the water in the pool was warm, but it was more a sense of peace. When I was under the water I knew from that moment on that my life was going to be different. I can't explain it – it was like the old me had just gone. I knew that all the doors to my past were closing and I didn't need to worry about it anymore, I could leave it where it is, in the past and move on with my life.

Two months later, after one of the church services Jimmy asked another parishioner, James if he would pray with me. We prayed together and afterwards we chatted about general things. We got on really well and the following Sunday we chatted again, but this time we were talking about anything and everything. Four hours later we were still sat in the church chatting, so we arranged to meet for a coffee another time. After that meeting we started seeing each other and five months later James proposed.

The old me never smiled because to me there was nothing to smile about. Now I can't stop smiling. People tell me I'm blooming. I feel a completely different person in such a small space of time. I've moved house, I've met new friends, I've been baptised, I've got engaged, I've stopped taking anti-depressants and my life is overflowing with good things. Don't get me wrong, I can still have bad days when I can get irritable and snappy, but I don't get down in the way I used to. If I find my mood is changing then I find something to do – I take the dog for a walk or go with my nephews to the park.

I still take one day at a time but the difference is, now I can see a future. I've got my confidence back and I am not afraid to go to new places on my own. I went to job club with someone from church. I've since had a few job interviews, and I am hopeful that I will be working soon.

When I look back it's hard to believe that I've come so far, from the person I was to where I am today. All I know is that I'm very thankful for all the people who have helped me, and for finding and accepting Jesus as my Lord. I have faith that he can work things out for good, even when I can't see how, and that's how I've decided to live.

4 'A full life'

Nick Barr-Hamilton

*'The thief comes only to steal and kill and destroy. I came
that they may have life, and have it abundantly.*

*I am the good shepherd. I know my own and my own
know me' (John 10:10, 14).*

John Sentamu writes:

'What does 'life in all its fullness' look like? Is it all about
money, friends, houses or cars? What happens when we
make our plans on the basis of goods that perish?

Nick felt robbed of his future when he lost the use of his
legs in a rugby injury. But as Nick's story unfolds, we see how
Jesus Christ was able to offer and reshape what 'life in all its
fullness' came to mean for him, and for others too.

Nick's experience demonstrates that the future does not
have to be defined by the past. With God, our future is filled

with all sorts of new possibilities rather than with problems. As Proverbs 16:9 says, *'The human mind plans the way, but the Lord directs the steps.'*

For God knows us; he knows our hearts, and the pains that we carry within, as well as the frailty of our bodies. He knows us and loves us, for who we are. Knowing that God loves us, and cares for us, no matter what, makes the impossible possible!

✠

Nick Barr-Hamilton's story:

I soon as I had my accident I was pretty sure what I'd done. I was lying on the rugby pitch after a freak tackle and my nose was touching my chest. I remember shouting lots of unrepeatable words while a nurse tried to calm me down. I wasn't not calm; I just knew that I was in trouble.

An ambulance arrived and I was taken to hospital where the staff cut off my rugby shirt, despite my protesting that they shouldn't wreck my top. I was told that I was being taken to surgery for an operation to relocate my neck. I was given a general anaesthetic and I don't remember much about the next two weeks after that.

I broke my neck just after my 16th birthday. I was at boarding school and doing what I loved to do, playing rugby. I loved being active. If I wasn't playing rugby on a weekend you'd catch me running up a mountain or doing some other outward bound activity. I had planned to join the Royal Marines as an officer, because it always seemed an exciting life. I'd even gone so far as to visit the forces recruitment office and sign up as a cadet. Now those hopes were well and truly shattered.

It was about three or four weeks after the accident when a doctor confirmed that I wouldn't be able to walk again. I had no idea what it meant to be partially paralysed for the rest of my life. In the months that followed I had pictures in my head of what that might look like. I imagined doing things but not being able to move around much. What I thought wasn't even vaguely close to the reality.

For the first eight weeks I was in traction, lying flat on the bed, unable to move anything at all. I then spent another four months in rehabilitation, and for some people with spinal injuries it is longer than that. I saw lots of people at that time who had spinal injuries from a number of causes. There were people who had fallen off bikes, fallen off horses, fallen off step ladders, people who had been crossing the road or who tripped over a kerb, and there were also a number of freak accidents that had no explanation whatsoever. I don't wish to sound fatalistic, but what happened to me could happen to anyone. Obviously if you participate in a lot of dangerous sports then you're more likely to get an injury of some sort, but the majority of spinal injuries are not sports injuries. I couldn't blame rugby for what happened to me. It was a choice I made, and you can't live your life fearing the worst.

I'm a stubborn person by nature and I decided early on that I was going to have to either give in or get on. I took my GCSEs from my hospital bed and after being discharged I went straight back to school to study for my A levels. My next step was university and I was offered a place to study natural sciences at Cambridge. I was looking forward to studying, living away from home and generally having fun, but things didn't turn out as I'd planned there either.

The first night at university I was heading towards to the bar area when a couple of guys, noticing that I was wearing a rugby shirt, asked if I'd like to join them for a rugby meeting. I thought, why not? I still loved the game and, just because I couldn't play anymore, I could go along as a supporter. One of the guys was a Christian, and after the meeting he asked if I'd be interested in coming along to what he called a 'Just Looking' group. I was, but not for the reasons he'd probably hoped. I wanted to go along to argue against the existence of God. I'd gone to church every Sunday at boarding school, but only because it was a school rule, and to get caught bunking off really wasn't worth the grief. After my injury I didn't want anything to do with a God who could let that happen to me. I wasn't a bad person, I was fairly 'moral' so why me? If there was a God, why didn't things like this happen to people who did terrible evil in the world?

So, I went along, but during that first year, as I read the Bible and learned more about Jesus, I began to run out of arguments. As a scientist I wanted to see the evidence, but all the historical evidence pointed to a real Jesus, which just left the question, is Jesus who he claims to be? I had to say, yes, because yes, the miracles did happen, and yes, Jesus was raised from the dead, which is ultimately what it hangs on. People say that miracles are impossible, but not if there is a God. Does that answer the question of suffering? No. Why doesn't God intervene more often? That's a hard one. I guess, I felt that he's shown us that he cares by coming into the world and suffering himself, and helping us to see that he knows what it's like to suffer. He also promises that he will make things right.

I'd had my intellectual arguments answered, but I don't think that made me a Christian. It was another six months before I made that choice. I went home for the summer and when I came back I fell in love for the first time. At the time, she was the most amazing girl ever, but when it all went wrong I found my hopes dashed again. I thought that there had to be more to life than this and was sitting putting the world to rights with a friend at one o'clock in the morning, as students do, when he said, 'Why don't you come along to church?' I realised that I was putting my hope in the wrong places, because these dreams offered no certainty of fulfilment. Knowing that the hope held out in the gospel was a certainty, I decided to give my life to Christ that night.

I'd like to say that after I became a Christian my life was transformed, that I stopped getting drunk and became a perfect person. Alas, it didn't happen like that, but my eyes were opened to more of the world around me. I stopped thinking of sin as something that's naughty but nice, and instead as something that causes damage to others, to the

world, and causes offence to God. I started to think about
how I was going to live my life and what I was going to do
after my degree from a different perspective. I thought about
what I was able to do, but it wasn't a case of just getting along.
I started to ask, what am I going to do with the gifts that I've
got and how can I best use my talents?

I left university with a good degree and took a summer job at
an investment firm in the city. I enjoyed it and thought I'd like
a job doing just that. The company offered me a four-month
contract, but I couldn't move all the way to London for four
months, so they suggested I go back the following year for a
graduate intake interview. After a year of being unemployed,
filling in more than 120 applications and attending dozens
of interviews, I returned to be considered for the graduate
intake.

I was interviewed by a former doctor, who was the first
person to ask about my disability. He really got to the practical
details of whether I was going to be able to do the job. Maybe
I got the job because he understood who he was employing
and could see that I was able to do it.

It was a good firm. I trained to be an investment manager,
passed all my professional exams and started managing multi-
million pound funds. I enjoyed my work. I met some really
interesting people, worked with lots of interesting companies
and got to travel to the USA a few times a year. Another
good thing about the company was that, unlike many city
firms, we didn't have to work long hours, which gave me the
time to get involved in my church, leading small bible study
groups and doing pastoral work. After four years someone
asked if I'd consider full time ministry? I talked to a couple of
people about it and decided that it definitely wasn't for me.
God had other plans. After six years of working in finance
there was a downturn in the city and I was made redundant.
By this time I could afford to work unpaid for a year, so I took
the opportunity to try full-time ministry.

I wrote off to a few people and ended up at a church in
Hull. That first year spent in ministry was the best of my life.

I was living in a horrible flat, but I didn't care because I was enjoying what I was doing so much. I loved mixing with people of all ages and feeling like I was making a difference to people's lives. I was having fun and I also felt a sense of purpose. The work made me realise that there are a lot of broken people, be it physically, emotionally, spiritually or financially. Having a faith in Jesus doesn't make people immune from any of these problems by any means, but I could see how it gives strength and takes away fear.

At the end of that first year, I thought, 'Yeah, this is what I want to do for the rest of my life.' I was persuaded to stay on in Hull for another year and applied for ordination. That same year I met and fell in love with Lucy. We married that summer and both went to theological college in September. I am now vicar of St George's Fatfield in the north east of England. Lucy and I have been married for eight years and we have a four-year-old daughter and a two-year-old son, who are both full of energy.

One of the reasons that I wanted to go into full time ministry was because I became aware of just how many people are suffering and finding life hard. I'm in a wheelchair, so it is obvious to other people that I can't walk, but I'm aware that there are a lot of people who have disabilities that aren't visible – mental health issues, or physical disabilities that are affecting their bodies in ways that can't be seen from the outside. Those people need help and support as well, and to be given hope and purpose for their lives.

Some people have said to me that I give them hope, as someone who can achieve despite difficulties. When I hear that, I usually mumble, 'I'm not that perfect,' but if I am an encouragement to others, then that is an encouragement to me too.

Even after I became a Christian, I was quite an angry person for a long time. Getting to where I am now was a slow healing process, but looking back I can see that God has had his hand on me all the way through, working through various people in my life.

There's no point in trying to paint a rosy picture of life when you've broken your neck – it sucks. Physically I get tired more easily and I still get frustrated by lots of things about my body that don't work and sometimes I wish they would. It takes me a lot longer to do things, so if I've got to go somewhere it takes me five minutes to get into the car and five minutes to get out again. Getting ready in the morning takes me between one and one-and-a-half hours, so I could never throw on some clothes and get out of the door in five minutes.

My life isn't easy, but then life is never easy. Like a lot of people after an injury, the first thing I thought about is what I can't do. I had to refocus and find out what I could do, take risks, and try new things. So, I've been skiing, kayaking, scuba diving, abseiling, sailing, shooting and I've been up Helvellyn, admittedly with some help. I don't do the same extreme sports now that I have children, but I enjoy being a dad, drinking a pint of real ale, getting out into the countryside, taking photographs, growing vegetables and cooking. My life is not what I imagined as a boy, but it is a full life, and while many of my earlier hopes have been smashed to pieces, others have exceeded my wildest dreams.

5 *'Everything in perspective'*

Jenna Gill

'The steadfast love of the Lord never ceases, his mercies never come to an end; they are new every morning; great is your faithfulness' (Lamentations 3:22-23).

John Sentamu writes:

The Book of Lamentations tells of the destruction of Jerusalem and the Temple. The surviving inhabitants had to flee or face the brutal rule of the occupying forces. Lamentations does not name its author, but it is generally attributed to the prophet Jeremiah who for many years warned people that by being unfaithful to God, there would be disastrous consequences.

Jeremiah's prophecies did not make him popular. Nevertheless when surrounded by death and destruction, he was quick to point out that God's loving kindness for each of us shines through.

Jenna's story is about responding in a similar kindness to those around her. She observed and put into practice that God's love, kindness and mercy are new every morning. With each new dawn, there is hope for what each day offers and those new possibilities are ever present. God never tires in his faithfulness.

As the truth of God's love and mercy permeates our lives we see the world with fresh eyes.

Jenna Gill's story:

When I was 18 I visited Tanzania with my church. I know it can sound corny to say the experience was life-changing, but for me it was. Of course, I didn't realise that until much later. I knew that the trip was an experience I would never forget, but it's only looking back that I can see how much it influenced my view of the world and as a result the choices I've made in my life.

At the time I'd been on holiday to Spain with my family, but I'd never travelled outside of Europe. I had heard about Issenyse School in Africa because my church, St Barnabas in Huddersfield, would often run fund-raising events to help raise money to support it. This particular year the church was organising a visit to the school and asked if any young people from the congregation would like to go. I was told what it was going to be like, but I don't think that you can be fully prepared for visiting somewhere so different, not at 18 years old anyway.

We knew that we were going to be working in a school, so we were all given different topics to learn and asked to prepare a lesson. My topic was malaria, so I did some research and found out that it is a preventable, life-threatening disease, which is transmitted by the bite of the female *Anopheles* mosquito. I also had statistics that informed me each year there are one million deaths from malaria worldwide, about 90% of which are in Africa. It was interesting, but it all felt quite remote until I got to Tanzania and began to sense what that means for the people living there. Before I arrived the information was just facts I needed to learn. Malaria sounded like a horrible disease but I was more worried about the idea of standing in front of a classroom and teaching. After all, I was still in school myself and I knew how cruel children could be to teachers. Until then, I'd never given much thought to how it must feel to stand in front of a class – it was nerve-racking.

I gave my lesson to a class of 80 children and when I started to speak they all looked at me with such expectation. There was no messing about, everyone in the room wanted to learn and their enthusiasm and attention took me by surprise. I realised how much I'd taken my education for granted. I'd been given a very good education for free and until that point it hadn't cost me a second thought. In a few months I would be going to university. I was thinking about getting the best job I could and earning as much money as I could. In comparison, the people my age in Tanzania wanted to be happy and safe, to see their brothers and sisters grow up and for them to have a nice life. I already had so much without even realising.

I didn't question my aims at the time, I still went to university with the idea of becoming a Doctor of Psychology and earning mega bucks listening to people's problems, but subconsciously something must have changed. I wanted to do something that would have a positive impact on the lives of others and so I began volunteering, at first with organisations helping refugees and asylum seekers and later with people who were homeless and vulnerable. I found I enjoyed this work more than my studies, and by the final year of my degree I knew where I wanted to be.

A couple of years after I graduated I got a job at Chapter 1, a charity, based on Christian principles, which specialises in providing accommodation and support for vulnerable people who might otherwise be sleeping rough or in insecure accommodation like sofa surfing. I work at a supported housing project in Liverpool, which can accommodate up to 53 men. Chapter 1 has a sister project called, TABS International, which stands for Together, Achieving, Believing and Sustaining. Its aims are two-fold: to raise funds to support sustainable education and community projects in Kenya, and to give disadvantaged young people from the UK a chance to work there as volunteers.

Just as I had benefited from the opportunity to volunteer in Africa before I went to university, the founder and chair of the organisation, Rachel Sanders had also seen the positive impact volunteering overseas had on her own children. I don't think that you could put anyone in that environment and it not have some sort of positive effect, but you need some support both emotionally and financially in order to do this kind of voluntary work. Rachel wanted to offer that opportunity to young people who wouldn't normally have the chance of such an experience because they don't have the necessary support behind them, and so TABS was born.

This year I went back to Africa with TABS. My focus was on supporting the clients, who were aged between 20 and 26, but whatever I gave on that trip I got back so much more in so many ways.

We were in Kenya for just under three weeks, working to extend a school that TABS had built in the heart of Thika's slum area. For safety reasons we couldn't stay in the slum. so we stayed in little huts outside and drove in every morning. We had spent time trying to prepare the young people for what it would be like. Of course, as it was for me, the reality is often quite different. At first there was a bit of grumbling because it seemed our living quarters were fairly basic and the food wasn't what we were used to. We were, however, staying in relative luxury – we had a meal cooked for us every day, hot water, and the use of a toilet with a seat.

On my previous trip to Africa, I hadn't seen slum dwellings where people erect makeshift houses out of mud, metal and any material they can get their hands on. There were big piles of waste and open sewers, the smell from which was overwhelming. All life was there in front of us in its rawest sense. There was no escaping it, even in the simplest of things. For example, if we wanted to eat chicken, we saw the chef grab a live chicken and serve it to us still looking like a chicken, not the fillets we're used to.

Most of us weren't used to physical labour either, and it was tough, especially in the heat of the sun. We worked with a local building company, which was important to us because we wanted to keep their economy going and make sure that the work we were doing was sustainable once we'd left. Our first job was to build the foundations for three new classrooms. It involved a lot of digging with not many spades, and the spades we did have were a bit old and dodgy. Once we'd dug the trenches we had several deliveries of huge stones, but because the truck couldn't fit round the back where we needed them we had to set up a production line to carry hundreds of stones from one place to another. We also had to mix cement from scratch because we didn't have a cement mixer. We'd get all the components of the cement, put it in a big pile and manually mix it together, which was difficult because if we used too much water or too much sand then it could all go horribly wrong. Thankfully, we had some expert help from the locals with that and then we put the stones together with the cement to build the wall. What might take half-an-hour in the UK would take us hours, but that was all part of what we were there to do and it felt great to be achieving something together.

While we were working some of the local people came over, picked up a spade and started helping. There was no question or expectation of them being paid, they just wanted to help their community. We didn't always speak each other's languages but we could communicate in a different way – we were all getting along together, we'd sit and eat lunch together and then get back to work. These people had nothing materially but they were happy to give everything. There was no moaning about how bad things are, they just used what they had and got on with it.

Once the foundations were in place the men from the building company erected the wooden frames and fixed on the metal panels, then added the finishing touches by painting it all blue. We also repainted the other school building and we dug out another drop toilet, so that they would have two.

While we were working in the slum we saw a lot of upsetting things and heard many sad stories. It was important for our group to be able to express some of that and let it go. So, every night after dinner we would have reflection time for people to talk about the things they'd seen or experienced during the day. We also talked about the good things, the many wonderful people who welcomed us into their homes and fed us. It also gave us time to reflect on our own lives. I missed people at home and realised just how many things in my life I take for granted. I'm probably a natural worrier, but I worry about silly things like if the washing up has been done. In Kenya I realised that I can spend too much time concerning myself with things that don't really matter. What matters is that people are happy and healthy, and that they are not struggling or living in a situation that is causing any kind of suffering. That's all so many people aim for in Kenya. They do try to better themselves, but it's not about getting the most money, rather it's about knowing that their children are happy and healthy and are going to school and getting an education. Everything is put in perspective when you meet people who are unbelievably grateful for every little thing they have, and are so welcoming – people who are just happy that you're there with them.

When we arrived the children sang for us. It was so lovely that we wanted to do something for them in return before we left. We made musical instruments out of plastic cups, beans and bells. All the children all got involved – it was great. Again it was about using what we had and realising that we had more than we might at first think. While we were out there we tried to play to the strengths of the young people. In the

UK they are underprivileged, but out there they realised that they have got skills and opportunities. One of the lads had a flair for music, so he made the instruments for our concert, one of the others was talented at painting so he was in charge of that work, and one of the girls was great with the children, so she helped out looking after the little ones.

In such a short space of time it was amazing to see a change in the young people and in how they had begun to talk about their lives. They all came away with new goals and the realisation that they do have choices and in that the power to change their lives for the better.

Towards the end of our trip one girl said to me: 'I don't get much money on benefits but these people here don't even have benefits. I have opportunities that I didn't even realise were opportunities. All my life I've blamed everyone else. I've blamed the job centre, I've blamed my mum, I've blamed friends, but being out here has made me realise that I have a choice and I need to take responsibility for my own life.' When we got home she started to do just that. She enrolled in college, got her own flat and is giving back by volunteering for an organisation helping young people with addictions.

For myself, I remember coming back the first week and thinking, we waste so much water and so much food, but that didn't last long. It's hard to change completely how we live. However, I do try to be more patient with people and to be the best I can in my job. On my return I looked into how I could better help TABS and have recently become a trustee, which means that I have a more active role in fundraising events. Although I don't always go to church every week, I feel that I have a different connection with God because of my experience. I've never felt as close to God as I did in Kenya. The church we went to there was a little tin shack, with no grand pictures on the wall or gold crosses. Yet, everyone put on their best Sunday clothes and looked so happy. They were all smiling and singing and dancing. Everyone loved God. We might say, God why don't you bring the rain so the people can eat? But there was never anything like that. All the people were praising God, confident that he would bring about good things in the end. They put their hope in God, and that's what really touched me.

6   'We've all got a direct line'

Elizabeth Pepper

He was praying in a certain place, and after he had finished, one of his disciples said to him, 'Lord, teach us to pray, as John taught his disciples.' He said to them, 'When you pray, say: Father, hallowed be your name. Your kingdom come. Give us each day our daily bread. And forgive us our sins, for we ourselves forgive everyone indebted to us. And do not bring us to the time of trial' (Luke 11:1-4).

John Sentamu writes:

Elizabeth's story of hope is all about the power of prayer and being totally reliant on God. What do you do when you feel there is nothing else you can do? Elizabeth tells us 'Don't just sit there, Pray something!' Wise words indeed.

Jesus starts his prayer with 'Father', a word of intimate reliance. His prayer unfolds to recognise that God's priorities come first, before the cry for our own needs and desires to be met. It also asks for us to be rescued from those times of trial.

Friends, The Lord's Prayer is not there just for recitation, it is rather a pattern of prayer to be lived out. For Elizabeth, this experience of prayer became very real in her helplessness, having to trust her husband to God and to others. Her story offers us an insight into this practice of prayer and how this can be ours too.

Prayer is a springboard – helping us to join in an already overflowing life-giving stream from the heart of God. As we join in, we realise that Jesus Christ and the Holy Spirit are already praying for us, with us, and in us, in ways that are too deep for words. Stillness and silence before God free us from fear and anxiety.

✢

Elizabeth Pepper's story:

I've always been a very anxious person. I suppose you'd say it's in my nature. If worry was an Olympic sport, I'd be up there with the medal winners. So, when my husband, Alan became ill you won't be surprised to hear that my worrying went into overdrive.

I first noticed he wasn't well when he started painting the ceiling in the sitting room and left it half finished. We are both retired, so it wasn't left unfinished because of a lack of time. Although he never complained, I knew than Alan wasn't up to doing the job. I'm not a medic, but you know when someone close to you isn't themselves, and Alan certainly hadn't been himself. He told me that he'd been having intermittent abdominal pain, which he'd mentioned to his GP, but because he didn't have any pain at the time of the appointment it was difficult for the doctor to work out what was wrong. I knew that it must have been bad for Alan to leave the decorating half finished, but we didn't know what it was, so I didn't say anything about his condition or the paint work. Later, when the pains starting interrupting his sleep, I became really worried. I had no idea what was wrong but I prayed that the pains would stop and Alan would be ok.

After a particularly restless night, I was up early, praying for Alan's healing, when I remembered a recent discussion at our Bible study group. We'd talked about how sometimes the answer to prayer lies within ourselves, in something we can do. I realised that there was something I could do. I called for medical assistance, and after I explained what was wrong an ambulance arrived to take Alan to Accident and Emergency.

At last it felt like we might get an answer, but when we arrived at the hospital the pains had gone, all his test results came back normal and it became really difficult to explain what was wrong.

'Please will you believe me when I say, I know he's ill?' I pleaded with the doctor.

I think that it was because of Alan's age, and because I couldn't manage him at home, that the doctor agreed to admit him. Once in hospital the staff began to see the symptoms we had tried to explain. Alan would spike a temperature and then he would be fine again. On the second day I was told that he had developed a fever. There was a bug in his system and the liver function test that had originally come back normal was now showing a change. The illness was still all very mysterious, until his condition worsened and surgery revealed an abscess on his liver.

Alan went into surgery a grey man, but after the abscess was drained he emerged from theatre with colour already back in his cheeks. I could hear him telling a nurse one of his awful jokes that I'd heard so many times before, and wouldn't have believed I'd feel so happy to hear once again.

When Alan was first admitted to hospital I called all my friends, my church and people on a prayer chain I was involved with, to ask for prayers for Alan's recovery and specifically that the laboratory staff would be able to identify the bacteria that was causing his infection, so that the doctors would know the right medication to give him. Knowing that all these people were praying for Alan meant a great deal to me, and I was delighted to be able to tell them that, although we still didn't know the cause of his infection, the cause of his pain had been identified and at last Alan was making progress.

I don't remember much of what happened after that, because my panic must have sent everything into a blur. Overnight, Alan took a turn for the worse. I must have had a phone call to tell me, but I don't recall. All I remember is walking along a hospital corridor towards the intensive care unit where Alan had been taken and seeing his surgeon walking towards me, then ushering me into a little room opposite.

The surgeon was very nice, but his words weren't ones that I wanted to hear. He said all kinds of things about complications and liver function. Things that I didn't understand. All I could take in was that Alan was going back to surgery and I had to prepare myself for the worst. The surgeon would do his best, but it was likely that Alan's kidneys would fail during the operation.

It was hard to take it all in. Alan's surgery was imminent. 'Has he got to go now?' The surgeon nodded and we walked together towards the intensive care room where Alan was lying. Everything was happening so quickly that I didn't have time to think and my words just tumbled out. 'But, he can't go to surgery without prayer, he must see the chaplain.' As I said it, I looked across the corridor and noticed a man standing there, wearing a red T-shirt. He looked familiar, and then I recognised who he was. 'Isn't that the Archbishop of York? Could you ask him to pray for Alan?'

'Talk about phone a friend,' the consultant said, 'have you got a direct line?'

I often think about those words because we all have a direct line, God is always there for us.

I left the consultant to speak to the Archbishop and I went into the room to see Alan. He was lying on a trolley and the staff were clearly in a hurry because he was ready to be moved to theatre. In a moment the Archbishop was there. He placed his hands on Alan and said: 'Alan, my friend.' Those words

meant so much to me. The Archbishop prayed and then Alan
was whisked away and I was shown back to the small room
where earlier I'd been told the news about Alan.

I'd been in a rush that morning so all I had with me was
my mobile phone and a pocket Bible. I rang my friend on the
prayer chain then the credit ran out on my phone so I couldn't
call anyone else. I began to read. It was hard to concentrate
but I just let the words wash over me. Then I knelt down and
prayed. I asked Jesus to help me and prayed that the Holy
Spirit would be with the surgeon and his team who were
operating on Alan. I was holding onto that thought when an
hour later a chaplain walked into the room. He was lovely
and I knew he'd come to support me, but I think I gave him a
rough time.

'Shall we pray?' he asked.

'What are we going to pray about?' I said. 'I can only pray
if we're going to continue to pray for healing.'

We discussed this for half an hour and then the door opened
and the surgeon walked in, still in his blue theatre scrubs. 'I've
managed to find the bleeding and I've managed to stitch it,'
he said.

It was incredible news. It was another two hours before I
could see Alan, but I was so thankful to have him back again.
The following day Alan was taken off the ventilator and when
I next spoke to the surgeon I was so excited.

'I'm afraid you haven't quite understood,' he said. 'When
I opened Alan I found that there was a problem with his bile
duct and there was nothing I could do to repair it. The only
thing I can suggest is that if he's well enough next week we'll
see if we can go in again.'

I had the weekend to sit next to Alan's bed. He was alive
and while I'm sure he was improving, the steps were so
small that it was difficult to appreciate them. The following
morning, the man in the bed next to Alan died. It suddenly
hit me, that the man being carried out of the ward could so
easily have been Alan and there was nothing I could do about
it if it were. I had no idea what would happen next. I was

completely dependent on the grace of God and the provision of the hospital staff.

That weekend I was very distressed, although I probably wouldn't have described it as such at the time. I probably would have said that I was panicking. I'd been home and was sat in the car outside my house ready to return to the hospital when suddenly I couldn't remember the simplest things about how to drive. I turned on the engine and needed to indicate but instead I turned the windscreen wipers on. I tried again. This time the back wipers started up as well, and the front ones were moving even faster. It seemed that the more I tried to remember what to do the more muddled I became. Eventually I managed to find the right switch and get the car going. I drove to the end of the road and as I turned the corner, I felt as if Jesus was in the car with me and everything was ok. I realise that sounds strange, but I can only tell it how it was. Nothing like that had ever happened to me before, I felt the most overwhelming sense of peace that it is very hard to articulate.

I can't explain what happened but know that I felt much more together after that. On the following Monday, Alan returned to surgery and again I waited in the same small room I had sat in nervously the week before. After 25 minutes one of the nurses came in and sat opposite me. Her face was serious. 'Your husband has had to be returned from surgery,' she said.

'Why, what's gone wrong?'

As it turned out, nothing had gone wrong, but to our amazement something had turned out more right than we could have hoped. The hole in Alan's bile duct had spontaneously reduced so significantly that there was no need to operate. In my eyes it was a miracle. In those past few days I'd seen God heal through the hands of the surgeon, through the understanding of the laboratory staff who found out which bacteria was causing the infection in Alan's blood, through the gift of medicine, and in unexpected ways that I can't explain.

I'm not the type of person who usually looks for things to be grateful for. Indeed at times I have definitely been a glass half-empty type of person, and could be quite bitter about opportunities I'd missed or about situations that I felt were unfair. Yet, over those few days I realised just how much I did have to be grateful for. There were all the people who supported me through prayer, the NHS and all it provides, and the wonderful people who give blood, often with little idea as to how important what they do is – Alan had to have so many blood transfusions and their gift kept him alive. I realised too, just how grateful I am for Alan and for the love we share. My thanks, even when I was able to find the people to express them, were quite superficial in comparison with how I felt.

Now life is much calmer again I try to hold on to those thoughts, along with all the reasons I can find every day to give thanks to God. I can't hand-on-heart say that I won't ever worry or even that I'll always be able to pull myself together quickly if I start to panic, but when I feel that happening I remind myself that Jesus is there for me, as he is for all of us. We've all got a direct line, if we just remember to use it.

7 'Lives can be transformed'

Stefan Heathcote

'All things come into being through him and without him not one thing comes into being. What has become into being in him was life and the life was the light of all people. The light shines in the darkness and the darkness has not overcome it' *(John 1:3-5).*

John Sentamu writes:

It was Christmas, 1939, at the height of the blitz when King George VI addressed the nation with this poem by Minnie Louise Haskins:

> *And I said to the man who stood at the gate of the year: 'Give me a light that I may tread safely into the unknown'. And he replied: 'Go out into the darkness and put your hand into the Hand of God. That shall be to you better than light and safer than a known way.'*

When Christ's light shines in our lives, we see the old familiar things in a new way. His light leaves no dark corners, and the darkness in us - blinded sight - cannot overcome it. Jesus Christ guides us as we go through storms, uncertainties and turmoil, so that we can reach safety.

Stefan's story shows us that in the midst of a chaotic life, he discovered that nothing is beyond God's power to make a difference, to transform what seems hopeless into hope. There are no dark places that His light cannot reach. With God's grace and light, we know that there is always a fresh start with God, and hope for the future.

✠

Stefan Heathcote's story:

Many people living difficult lives believe that nothing they can do will change their circumstances. They don't see the opportunities open to them to live a better life. For a long time I was one of those people.

Looking back my life was very messy. Of course, I didn't see it like that at the time. It was my life, it was how things were. After all, wasn't life supposed to be messy on the Moss Rose Estate in Macclesfield?

When I was 12 years old I was suspended from school 45 times in one year, and because that was the maximum number of times allowed, the next time I got into trouble I found myself permanently excluded. After that, I was given one-to-one tuition for a few months. Eventually I was offered a place at another school, but it didn't last long. A couple of weeks later I got into a fight with a teacher and was permanently excluded again.

For some people, being permanently excluded from school twice in less than as many years would be serious, but I wasn't bothered. I didn't like school anyway. I didn't like being told what to do and when to do it. I struggled with the work, which didn't help, but more than that I couldn't see the point in school. Even if I took my exams, what would it matter? There were no jobs anyway. No jobs for people like me, people from the Moss Rose Estate.

So, at 13 years old I decided that school had nothing to offer me and I wasn't going back. I was classed as a school refuser, which basically means that I stayed at home and found other ways to keep myself entertained.

By the age of 15 I was making £200 a week selling cannabis and the odd bit of cocaine. Although I sold drugs, I never took them myself. I'm not sure why, maybe it was because cannabis smelt a bit weird or probably more likely because none of my close friends did. I had a group of five close friends and, while we drank plenty, we never smoked tobacco or anything else.

I knew that selling drugs was illegal, but I wasn't worried about that. I always imagined that I'd spend some time in prison one way or another, that I'd be like my older brother. I was 11 when I first visited my brother in prison. Again some people might think that experience would have put me off any criminal activity, but it didn't. I enjoyed going. We'd all get in the car and drive to the prison together – it was a day out.

When I started drug running, £200 sounded like a lot of money, but I soon spent it buying food for me and my friends. I bought a motorbike too and used to ride up and down the estate annoying the other residents. That was until I set my younger brother on fire. It was an accident. I was filling the bike up with petrol from a can and it caught light. I kicked it away, it splashed petrol on my brother and the next thing I knew he was alight too. Thankfully he's ok now, but he was in hospital for three weeks to treat the burns and when he came out he was all covered in bandages and looked like a mummy. I got rid of my bike after that.

There were a lot of crazy things at that time, like when the armed response unit came out because we were firing air rifles at people's houses and made us lie face down on the road. I guess the only peace I knew was when I was fishing. Sometimes I'd stay out all night. It would be very cold but I didn't mind that because it was so peaceful. I liked catching the fish too, but that didn't happen very often, so it was more the peace of being by the river that I enjoyed.

It was about the same time that I first got involved with the Cre8 project. Cre8 is a Christian organisation that believes people's lives can be transformed by building community, and by treating each other with care, forgiveness and respect. Its vision is to help people to free themselves from things that hold them back in life like poor health, damaged relationships and unemployment, and to help them gain access to education, training and work, as well as building friendships and having fun. I didn't know or understand any of that at the time. It was based in a house opposite where I was living and I just went over to be nosy. Well to be honest, I wasn't in school and was making a nuisance of myself because I had nothing better to do. I'd throw things at the people working at Cre8 from across the road, wind them up and generally get under their feet.

One day some older guys from my street were doing some work there, so I wandered over to see how they were getting on. They were building a shed and asked if I wanted to help. I wasn't doing anything else so I thought, why not? After that I got invited to some clubs they were running. There were about 20 other young people from the estate and we'd play games and do crafts. I was very keen on the craft side, particularly origami and model making. I learned practical skills, like mending bikes. From that I got into cycling and a group of us cycled coast to coast, from Workington to Tyneside.

I was really enjoying myself and I even let one of the supervisors, Jonny, persuade me to start doing some school work again. I didn't go back to school, but Jonny and his wife Angie got in touch with my old school and started teaching me in the Cre8 house. I never thought I'd be able to get any exams, but to my surprise I managed to pass two GCSEs in English and Maths.

As time went on, running drugs made less and less sense to me, so I lied and pretended I was 16 so that I could apply for a job at a recycling plant. That was fine until one day my older brother showed up. We got into a fight about money and I was sacked. I didn't want to go home after that. I'd made up my mind I was going to live on the streets when Jonny said I could move into their spare room for a while. I didn't feel I knew him that well, but it had to be better than sleeping rough, so I agreed.

Jonny and Angie went to church, so to be polite I went along too. At first I wasn't really interested in the church side of it, but they had a youth club and I enjoyed going to that. It felt good to be around other sensible young people. Not that I was a sensible young person. When I first went along I felt totally different and thought I wouldn't fit in, but everyone was so friendly. We went to Christian concerts and camps together and I made some great friends. I think it helped that they didn't know my background, although it felt at times as though I was living two lives. After a while people started asking questions about my past. I always told the truth and the people were still my friends, but I'm not sure how much they believed – they said they couldn't imagine me like that. I suppose I had changed. I wasn't running drugs for a start, doing that didn't make sense to me anymore. I didn't want the hassle and I certainly didn't want the fights.

There wasn't one definite thing that shifted in my mind to make me think that I could do something with my life. I think it was just a mix of all the positive things that went on after I moved in with Jonny.

In those couple of months, Jonny and Angie started talking to me about going to college. Now that definitely wasn't me, or so I thought. I didn't even go to school so how could someone like me go to college? I laughed it off at first but I could tell that Jonny really thought it was possible and eventually I started to believe it too.

We started talking about what I would do if anything was possible and I told him about helping out on my grandparents' sheep farm when I was growing up. If I could do anything I'd work as a sheep farmer, but the farm was sold when my granddad died, so I didn't see any chance of that happening. Jonny didn't agree that it was impossible.

Now my life was calmer I was able to move back home with my mum. I kept in touch with Jonny and he helped me to enrol on a course to learn animal care. It took me one-and-a-half hours to get to college in the morning, but I didn't mind because I liked what I was doing. A couple of months into the course I got moved onto a higher level of study and then a year after that I was accepted to study agriculture. I couldn't believe it.

After college I took a year out and started a student placement with Cre8. That same year I got the opportunity to visit Nepal for ten weeks with another organisation called Platform 2. There were about 30 of us, all aged between 18 and 25, and our project was to help build a school. It was an amazing experience. I lived with a family and was able to help out on their farm, milking the cows by hand and helping to harvest the rice. It made me appreciate how well people live in England – we can just nip to the shop and get whatever we need without thinking about it.

The following year I got my first job on a farm, feeding livestock and driving tractors. It was hard work and long days, starting at 4am and not finishing until 7pm. It was especially tough getting up at that time of the morning when it was frosty, but I was good at it and I think that everyone could see I was good at it.

I was doing everything I'd always wanted to do but when I imagined working on the farm for the rest of my life I wasn't so sure that it was still my dream. About the same time, Jonny contacted me. He was leaving Cre8 and his job would be coming up as Cre8 Works Supervisor. Cut a long story short, I got the job and that's what I'm doing now.

The project, part of Cre8, is a social enterprise that works with young people to develop the skills they need to find employment. Basically, I'm working with people, like myself, to encourage them to gain work experience or to get back into some kind of education. Since I've been involved my younger brother has gone to college through the Cre8 Works programme and still helps out at the project a couple of days a week.

I've lived on the Moss all my life, and most of the workers at Cre8 live on different streets of the estate, so we know what's going on and which kids aren't in school. When I first try to help someone I might get a swear word and told to go away, but those same kids see me around every day, so they know that I'm not going to go away. Eventually they'll come over and have a chat and I just work on building that relationship. They tell me, there's no jobs or they won't be good at college – all the same things that I thought when I was their age. When I'm tired I can think the job's a nightmare, but on a good day, when I've got loads of energy then I really enjoy helping them.

I still do a bit of farming. I've rented a field in the next town and have five sheep on it. It's a hobby really, but I love to go and sit there, where it's nice and peaceful. Sometimes I take the young people from Cre8 to watch my dogs run with the sheep. I do it to show them that their life is not all about what they're doing now, that they do have choices, and that life can be good on the Moss.

8   *'Learning to like ourselves'*

Ann Sunderland

'Behold I am making all things new' (Revelation 21:5).

John Sentamu writes:

Sometimes, even with wisdom and discipline, life just doesn't work out the way that we plan! Unjust and unfair situations can make life feel like hard work. We all make mistakes and the choices we make can leave us isolated. Things can go so badly wrong that it feels impossible to find a way back.

Sometimes in meeting others we get a sense of their tragedy, pain and alienation which seems too much to endure. But we also marvel at how the Christian virtue of hope held them firm in the storms they faced. It was a matter of clinging on to God. And they discovered that God, Father, Son and Holy Spirit, is holding on to them.

Ann's story is about longing for and finding restoration. The promise that Jesus offers is that He's making everything new for us. For whatever life throws at us, whatever storms we face, He is our anchor.

In Jesus Christ there is forgiveness for all past wrongs, new life for the present and hope for the future. With the Holy Spirit at your side, everything is possible!

✣

Ann Sunderland's story:

Do you ever look at someone else's life and think if only I had their house, job, holidays, relationship, clothes, looks or whatever, then I'd be happy? If you have, you might have looked at me and thought, she has a good life. In many ways you would have been right, but it didn't feel like that to me at the time. I had everything I thought I'd ever wanted, only to find that I didn't want any of it.

From the outside my life seemed fantastic. On the inside, life was a living hell. I'd look in the mirror and dislike everything about my appearance. I didn't want to be me anymore. It was frightening to realise that there was nothing in my life that I valued. I didn't want my relationship, I didn't want my house, I didn't want my business – I didn't want anything.

Looking back it's not easy to see where things started to go wrong, when my partner Paul and I went from enjoying a drink to becoming problem drinkers. I had convinced myself that drinking two or three bottles of wine each night was all part of our successful lifestyle. I liked good living and I'd often do things to excess. I didn't see our drinking as a problem because it never affected our ability to work, we never drank before 4pm, and we never drank for any reason other than we liked to drink and we could drink.

Our life was about making money and having fun. In business we were doing well. We ran a clothing shop that had managed to survive two recessions. If we ever felt fed up we'd just book a holiday and get away. We'd tell ourselves that it was a trip to buy stock for the shop, but when we got there we'd spend a small amount of time buying stock and the rest of the holiday having fun and drinking. For us, drinking was fun and we were drinking partners. Then somewhere along the line it stopped being fun. I remember packing my case for a business trip and making sure that I'd left enough room for the bottles. It wasn't the first time I'd done this, but suddenly it hit me that everything we did was planned around drinking and it wasn't healthy. Something had to change. I knew then that either I was going to stop drinking or I was going to kill myself doing it, so I stopped. Unfortunately, at the time, Paul didn't feel the same.

There had been times in the past when I would try to get us to stop drinking for a while. I'd find it quite easy to stop but usually Paul would want to get back into it and, feeling like I was missing out, I'd join him. This time was different because when Paul tried to coax me back into drinking I wasn't going to be swayed. It was unusual to choose to do something without Paul because we had always been so close – we spent all our time together, both at home and at work. In some ways it was difficult to know what was the bigger problem, alcohol or co-dependency. We'd got ourselves into a bubble where we didn't trust anyone else and soon we didn't trust each other either.

We tried relationship counselling both separately and together, but the truth was we were no longer in the same place in our lives anymore. I wanted to change and I had changed. Paul saw my wanting to clean up my lifestyle as wanting to move away from him. He became verbally abusive towards me and there were regular threats of violence and suicide. He would calm down for a while and then just as I'd begin to trust him something else would happen that he couldn't control and the abuse would start again.

We both joined support groups and for a time I convinced myself that I could cope and that I could help Paul to give up the drink too. Then, just as I'd think I'd pulled Paul round, he'd go back into a downward spiral and drag me down with him. He had it in his head that I didn't love him, that I was treating him badly and trying to manipulate him. Our lives were punctuated with this craziness and it was breaking me down to the point where I felt like I was losing my mind. The idea of separating from Paul seemed like the worst thing that could happen in my life, but once I realised that I couldn't save him, I felt like I had no choice.

When I walked out on our relationship after 12 years together, I truly thought that was it – there was no going back. It was the hardest thing I had ever had to do, but once I'd made the break things started to calm down. We were both attending support groups that had a spiritual basis and had begun to pray. For me, prayer offered a small glimmer of light at the end of the tunnel and slowly I felt like I was getting my sanity back. I began to notice a change in Paul too. I felt safer talking to him and it was clear that he had started on a spiritual journey. He talked about Jesus and about an Alpha course he was thinking of doing. I was intrigued by this change in him. Paul's dad was an atheist and his dad's dad was an atheist, so he had grown up convinced that there was nothing out there. Indeed at one point Paul was really anti-religion. If anyone had ever suggested anything like an Alpha course he would have said, 'Leave me alone, don't ever tell me about anything like that, I don't want to know' – although perhaps he wouldn't have said it quite as politely.

I believed in God, but Jesus was a mystery to me. I didn't know anything about him. I'd always held the same view as Paul that Christians were a bunch of boring weirdos. Now, after seeing such a positive change in Paul, my view was changing. I'd like to go on something like the Alpha course Paul was talking about, I thought, but after everything that had happened I didn't know if I trusted him.

Talking about God and Jesus kept us feeling safe. Even though we were still both in a lot of pain, it felt as though we were moving in the right direction. Gradually our relationship started to re-build, but on a different basis. This time God was at the centre holding us together and we knew that without him we wouldn't have a relationship.

Paul and I were apart for three months. Looking back it feels as if God was saying to us, 'Right, you go over there, and you go over there, so I can sort you out and then bring you back together.' We were committed to praying because we knew God was saving us both, so when the chance to join an Alpha course came up again we both jumped at it. It was exciting to explore our faith together and I realised that it wasn't just Paul who was changing for the better, I was changing too. My heart was softer and I wasn't so afraid.

When the vicar got to know us he said to Paul, 'Have you ever asked Ann to marry you?' Paul had asked me years ago. I didn't want to be married then. In the past I'd felt repulsed when women said: 'Your wedding day is the best day of your life.' I'd never wanted to be married in my life and could never understand how anyone could say that. Hearing the vicar ask Paul, I realised that my views had changed, that I had changed and that I would like us to be married. That was in May. By the end of June we were husband and wife. At one time I would never have believed I'd hear myself say it, but our wedding day was the most enjoyable day of my life – I felt in a state of bliss for about a week afterwards.

It wasn't just being married that I started to feel different about. I started to enjoy everything in my life more than I could ever remember. We'd had our business for ten years but we'd never wanted to work in the shop ourselves. We always had staff doing that for us so that we could be out enjoying ourselves. The reason for that was partly because we didn't much care for other people. In fact we were terrified of people we didn't know because we didn't trust anyone. Once I started to put my trust in God I didn't worry as much about trusting people. I felt safe knowing that God would guide me and that safety enabled me to begin to reach out to other people and start to build relationships. It gave me a great freedom, which allowed me to enjoy being in the shop and meeting new people. My work stopped being all about money and more about how I could provide a good service and help other people.

I was working for God, not for myself. That realisation was liberating because I didn't have to feel so responsible all the time. I'd do my best and if for any reason the business failed, I knew that God would have something else lined-up for me. Of course, it's not always as simple as that. Life still has its ups and downs. Not every day is brilliant but when things get tough and I'm getting into my old pattern of worrying, I remind myself that I don't need to panic because in God I've got a Father who can sort things out for me. I don't need to battle through or work it out for myself. I need to let go and trust that God has a solution to every problem. I've learned to never lose hope, no matter how old I am or how much I think a part of my life is over, because God loves me and is working for my good, even when I can't see it.

In that way I'm learning to be okay in my suffering too. In times of pain I reach out to God and it brings me closer to him. Instead of feeling sorry for myself I think, what can I learn from this? I know God is making me stronger through my pain and more compassionate, because sometimes I feel so happy that I think how can I help people who are hurting when I can't remember what that feels like myself? I might be struggling with a cold, but then I think about people who are really suffering and it softens my heart and makes me more eager to do something to help others where I can.

My life now is like a dream come true. For too many years we'd worshipped drink, now we have put God back in his right place – at the centre of our lives and our relationship. Neither of us drink alcohol anymore and we don't want to either. I'd never have believed it, but we can be around other people drinking and that's fine, it doesn't bother us.

An even bigger blessing is that we've seen our relationships restored with our families. We'd been so self-absorbed for such a long time that we'd completely disregarded family and friends. We'd even stopped seeing Paul's two children from his previous marriage regularly because getting them back to their mum's had become a pain when we were drinking. It is so wonderful that they have welcomed us back into their lives with such pleasure and love. I think they are amazed at the change in us; we are like different people to them and they can't believe it. It's taken a while to get used to it ourselves. Jesus has changed all our principles and values, we can't ever deny that because we couldn't have done this by ourselves. He's shown us who we are meant to be and we're not the people we thought we were. We're learning to like ourselves and realising that we're quite nice people really.

Now when I look in the mirror I think, 'Yeah, I'm ok and it can only get better'. I thank God every day for everything we've been given in our lives. I don't know what the future will bring or where God is taking us, but it's an exciting journey, and I can't wait to see what happens next.

9　'Our hope in his hands'

Dianne Skerritt

'I was naked and you gave me clothing, I was sick and you took care of me, I was in prison and you visited me.' Then the righteous will answer him, 'Lord, when was it that we saw you hungry and gave you food, or thirsty and gave you something to drink? And when was it that we saw you a stranger and welcomed you, or naked and gave you clothing? And when was it that we saw you sick or in prison and visited you?' And the king will answer them, 'Truly I tell you, just as you did it to one of the least of these who are members of my family, you did it to me' (Matthew 25:36-40).

John Sentamu writes:

How do we see people? Dianne's story is about seeing people's different needs and conditions, and not treating them as 'the other'.

Whilst we might cry out to God for help in appalling situations around us, in this parable and through Dianne's example, we are reminded that sometimes God will use us to 'be the change we want to see'.

Sometimes the need can seem overwhelming and we have no idea where to start. But, Dianne started where she was at.

Putting ourselves into the shoes of others is hard.   It's actively looking for and seeing someone else as a stand-in for Jesus Christ. It is about recognising need and being willing to make a difference. Trusting and obeying Jesus Christ doesn't just make the difference on a personal level, it means recognising that everybody, absolutely everybody, is created in the image of God, and is therefore of infinite worth.

The systems we create may sometimes forget that we are dealing with real people. This is something Dianne has never forgotten. By doing everything possible to make the change for one person, this in turn makes the difference for countless others.

Dianne Skerritt's story:

Growing up in Barbados, I was very aware of the gulf between rich and poor. Where I lived there were a lot of people struggling to make ends meet. You could spot them straight away because their shoes had holes in, or their trousers were ripped. The houses they lived in didn't have a kitchen. They had one living area and in the corner were three stones with a pot on top, and that's where they cooked. I didn't know much else about them. All I knew is that they were poor, and on this fact alone they were judged.

My gran would always give to these people. In many ways she was very generous and if she could help out materially then she would. People would come to our door and she'd give them money, or food, or goods, but she would never let me go through their door. I could never play with the children from those families.

'Dianne, if you keep company with those people, no one from a decent background will want to marry you,' my gran would say.

I was 15 years old at the time and getting married was the last thing on my mind. I was concerned, however, about being told what to do. To a certain extent my gran's rules were my rules because I lived with her and my granddad, and they had brought me up. Nevertheless at 15, I had my own mind and my own ideas about life, especially when it came to who I could and couldn't be friends with. Barbados was very class driven, and that never sat very easily with me.

'If you don't stop keeping company with people I don't like I'm going to send you to your mother in England,' my gran threatened.

I didn't believe her. I was the only grandchild living at home at the time, and my gran had brought me up, I never for a moment thought that she'd let me go. Then one day she called my bluff. I got home from school to find an envelope addressed to me on the library table and inside it was my plane ticket to the UK. I had two weeks to pack up and go.

'You'll love it when you get there, Dianne,' my teacher told me, 'You'll have scones and afternoon tea in the garden, it will be wonderful.'

My mum was living in Preston, Lancashire with my step-dad. We never had afternoon tea on the lawn. We didn't even have a bathroom and the toilet was at the top of the garden. This wasn't what I was used to. In Barbados we were well off. We had women who came and took our washing, we had a gardener and we also had a yard boy, who did whatever the gardener told him to do.

I cried every night for six months at the unfairness of it all. Not only was I now learning what it felt like to be poor, but I was a minority within a minority. The other people I met in the UK who were from Caribbean Islands had been running from poverty, they hadn't lost their home comforts, they hadn't been sent away, as I saw it, to be punished.

'Do you remember back home when you used to have holes in your shoes?' the other Caribbean girls would say. 'And do you remember when you went to the standpipe for water?' I didn't remember those things, because for me they never happened. At first I'd tell the truth and say: 'Not really, because I didn't come from a family who went to the standpipe for water.' By saying that it became clear I wasn't one of them and I'd get ostracised from the group. In the end I lied and said: 'Yes, I remember carrying water on my head.' Of course I didn't, that was never my experience, but I quickly became aware of the injustices and judgements on both sides, rich and poor. From that awareness sprung a sense of wanting to do right by every person regardless of their background, and it is something that has stayed with me.

I'm now 66 years old and I know that in many ways society has moved on, for the better. Some things haven't changed, however. There are still rich and poor, there is still injustice in the world, and I am still doing my part to try to create a world where people are treated equally and with respect.

I was employed for many years in social work. I'd recently retired when a job came up at The Rainbow Project in Nottingham. There were two strands to the job. The first was promoting racial equality and cultural diversity, which I knew a lot about from my previous roles. The second was providing advocacy, practical and spiritual help for people seeking sanctuary and refugees, a population I knew very little about.

At first when my friend told me about the job I had no interest, I was just turning 60 and in my head I'd finished with work. I told my friend this but she insisted I would be ideal for the job and that I'd also enjoy it. She nagged me about it and I resisted until every barrier I put up gave way and I resigned myself to the fact that I might as well fill in the application form. From that moment it was as if everything worked in my favour to get the job. Whatever obstacle I put in the way people would find ways around it. For example, my car was in the garage which meant that I couldn't get to the office to collect the application form so my brother-in-law offered me a lift; I didn't fill the form in on time but there was a postal strike so the recruiters accepted a late application; I couldn't take the job straight away because my dad was ill and I had to fly to New York to be with him and I was told that if I accepted the post they would wait nine months for me to start. Nine months! No one agrees to that, or at least I didn't think they would. I laughed to myself – sometimes things are just meant to be, and there's no point fighting against it. No matter what I said, it seemed that there was no getting out of this job, so I flew out to New York and agreed to come back and start the job in two months.

If I was going to do this job, I wanted to do it properly, which meant getting up to speed quickly with all things to do with asylum. I knew that everything I read in the media about immigration and asylum wasn't true. As with all things in life, you will get people who are abusive and take advantage, unfortunately. There are genuine asylum seekers and there are bogus ones. Some of the stories in the papers may be true, but they aren't true of all asylum seekers. Yet, it in many ways dealing with asylum seekers felt like going back to the days of my youth. These were the poor people that we had already made a decision about without talking to. The term 'asylum' was loaded with so many judgements about a person without knowing any details of his or her personal situation.

We hear a lot in the news about people who are falsely claiming asylum. But recently we are hearing the stories of people who flee genuine persecution only to be treated as criminals when they arrive on our shores. Until I took on this role, I wasn't aware just how awful the situation is for some of the asylum seekers once they are in the UK. As I speak, investigations are going on into alleged sexual abuse of vulnerable women detained at Yarl's Wood Immigration Centre. If the accusations are upheld, these are women who have fled abuse in their own country only to find more abuse in a place where they believed they would be safe. They have fled from one atrocious situation into another. If people have escaped torture and are on the verge of being deported back into that situation they will grasp at anything. Where is the hope in that? Yet, for many of the people I work with, hope is all they've got left. When everything has been stripped away, all they have left is faith and hope in a better future – a belief that no matter how bad things get, there is something better at the end.

In this job I get to see that change – to see good come out of what first appears to be a hopeless situation. Recently, we had a client referred to us whose case was being heard in Nottingham. Until then she was being detained in Yarl's Wood Immigration Centre, where she'd been living for six months. The woman was from the Congo and had entered the country on a false Belgian passport, a crime for which she'd spent three months in prison. She didn't speak any English, so I took a case worker with me who spoke fluent French to act as a translator.

After my initial visit I couldn't sleep. This woman appeared to me to be in her late 70s and was genuinely running from a war, which had already claimed the life of her husband. In my view she had suffered enough without being held in a detention centre, but there was no one who would bail her. So, the next day in work I asked: 'Why can't we bail her?'

'We don't put up bail for people, we're a project,' I was told.

'But what's to stop us from trying?'

The Reverend agreed that we could put the surety up, but we would need an address to bail her to, because an office address wouldn't be accepted by the court. Not to be deterred, I spoke to some people from our local Congolese community who agreed to find someone who would provide a bail address if they could meet with my client. We'd never done anything like this before and took a risk that the woman would try to escape. Thankfully everything went through smoothly and the woman was granted asylum.

Two months later I was in church when a very slim, elegant woman in her late forties approached me.

'Hello,' she said, as if I should know her. 'Don't you remember me?'

It was the client from the Congo. Once she said her name, I knew who she was, but she was unrecognisable from the woman I first saw. The woman I first met was so distraught and full of despair that she appeared to me to be an old woman, and an unhealthy one at that. Now, here she was with her hair swept back beautifully, looking chic and healthy – the transformation was wonderful to see.

Moments like that are what have kept me in this job for seven years, when I originally thought I'd last no more than one. I've stayed because the work is interesting, challenging and brings me in contact with some lovely people. I've had some very good jobs in the past, but I can confidently say that this is the best job I've had. I don't feel I'm in the job on my own, because some of the changes I've seen at one time seemed impossible. There was one family we were working with from Pakistan for whom all hope of being granted asylum seemed lost. The family was being detained in Yarl's Wood and deportation was imminent. I kept thinking that there must be one more thing we could do, and there was: we could pray. We held a vigil one evening and people from all nationalities and religions in the community joined us. It was incredible to see everyone come together to support this family. The event led to their case being reviewed and in time that family was granted asylum and is now settled in a new home. In that case it really felt like we'd had divine intervention. We could ask, why does God intervene sometimes and not others? When I think about that and about my own experiences it leads me to believe that God probably intervenes all the time without us realising. Only sometimes his help is more visible, because we know that there was nothing left to do, but to put our hope in his hands.

10 'All I had to do was ask'

Joanne Gibbs

Thomas said to the other disciples, 'Unless I see the mark of the nails in his hands, and put my finger in the mark of the nails and my hand in his side, I will not believe' (John 20:25).

John Sentamu writes:

It is a life-changing experience when you suddenly realise that this Jesus Christ person who you have heard about is actually real. And that He is able to do things in the real lives of real people. I guess that we will have heard the story of so-called 'doubting Thomas' who refused to believe that Jesus had really been raised from the dead until he had seen and touched his wounds for himself. To hear that Jesus Christ 'is Risen' second-hand wasn't good enough.

We may have heard about Jesus. We may even know people who say that they have encountered this Jesus. But until we know him and experience his reality for ourselves, it can all seem like just another story. Fine for others, but not for me.

It is when we have an encounter with Jesus, like 'doubting Thomas' – or like Joanne in this chapter - that suddenly everything is different. Jesus becomes more real than our very next breath. Jesus invites us to walk with Him, and promises that He will walk with us. And like Thomas, and like Joanne, we respond *'My Lord and my God'*, knowing that life will never be the same again.

Joanne Gibbs' story:

It is very easy to look at how someone else is living their life and point a critical finger. I know, because for many years I was that person standing in judgement of anyone who was different. I believed that my way was the only way. I'd criticise people without knowing them, and I wasn't interested in hearing other points of view. In my mind, I was very much in control of my life and I couldn't understand people who for whatever reason didn't have it all together.

My husband Dean and I had built up an electrical business and were enjoying a lot of success. We had worked hard to grow our business into a national company, and it was brilliant to feel that we had created that situation. Our life was always ordered and planned. In our kitchen you would find the same number of knives and forks in the cutlery drawer, all facing the same way. Everything had its place and that was how we lived.

I suppose you could say that our relationship was part of the order of things as we'd made them. Dean and I were very much 'team Gibbs'. We worked together and we played together. We never did anything separately, and we never wanted to. Perhaps we could have carried on that way quite happily, but as we know, life doesn't always work out as planned, so when Dean was diagnosed with renal cancer at the age of 47, suddenly neither of us felt in control.

I very much wanted to be the strong one, to hold everything together for the rest of the family, but at the same time I couldn't imagine how we'd ever get through this. I couldn't see any future, because there was nothing to look forward to. All I could think was, 'This is it! Everything I've ever known has ended'. As far as I was concerned, my life was finished.

Thankfully the doctors were more optimistic. Dean had a kidney removed and after a few months of recovery there was no evidence that his cancer had spread. 'You can go and get on with your life,' the consultant said. So, that's what we did, although we could never forget about what had happened. Dean bounced back well, but the thought of the illness was always there in the background, and our fears would come to the fore every time he had a scan or a test.

I tried to coax Dean into taking it easier at work, but that just led to more frustration. The business was his drive and it was hard to get him to step back from it. Soon he didn't have much choice in the matter, because a year later we discovered he'd a heart defect from birth, which was now causing problems and meant that the valves in his heart needed to be replaced.

Again, Dean was straight back to work after the operation. The business had always been so much a part of our lives, mine for ten years and Dean's for at least ten years before that. If a buyer hadn't approached us, I'm not sure we would have thought about selling, but when the opportunity arose it seemed like the right time. We'd given so much of ourselves to the company, now it was important to focus on getting Dean well.

After all of Dean's health scares, living a healthier life was becoming important to both of us. We both needed to lose weight and get fit, so we started walking together and after about eighteen months we had lost ten stones each and were feeling the benefits. Life was good again. Dean got a new job as a business development manager, the boys were settled at university, and five years after his original diagnosis, Dean's test results showed he was clear of cancer. It was brilliant news – we could start making plans again. So, at the end of that same month we did something we'd always dreamed of doing: we moved to York.

We had been in York two days when Dean became ill again. We were unpacking boxes in the living room when he tried to stand and he couldn't. 'I can't feel my legs,' he said.

'Oh it's probably pins and needles the feeling will come back', I said, unconcerned.

I thought he must have been kneeling on the floor in a strange position, but when the feeling didn't come back it was clear there was something more serious going on. Dean was rushed to hospital and within a matter of hours was transferred to another hospital for emergency surgery to remove a mass on his spine. Unfortunately the position and spread of the tumour meant that it wasn't possible for the surgeon to remove it completely. Dean survived the operation, but he was left paralysed from the chest down, and the prognosis was that he wouldn't live to see the end of the year. You might expect that the months that followed were our darkest, but something wonderful and unexplainable happened to Dean during that time, and the change in him sparked a change in me, filling me with a hope that I never could have dreamed possible.

I first noticed a change in Dean when he was recovering from surgery. He said he'd had a spiritual experience, but was quite confused about it because it went against everything he believed. Dean had never had any religious belief. As far as he was concerned the idea of God was a load of mumbo-jumbo – and at times he could be quite vocal about that, to the point of being offensive. After talking to other people, Dean put his experience down to having a lot of anaesthesia and strong medication, but when it happened again two months later, he was convinced there was something more and asked me if we could go to church so he could explore it further.

I was surprised by the turnaround in Dean's belief, but at the same time I was pleased he had a new focus and was looking forward to life with excitement again. Physically he could do very little and was reliant on other people to wash him and do everything from a personal point of view. We had to rely on care assistants and hoists to get him out of bed, and it could take up to four hours to get him through his morning routine and into the wheelchair. Yet, all those practical hardships aside, I can't begin to tell you about the fun and laughs we had at that time.

Dean insisted that we go into town every day. We'd spend hours in coffee shops and if Dean saw someone sitting alone at a table he would instigate conversation, something he never would have done in the past. Although Dean was restricted physically in what he could do to help people, he had a wonderful ability to make people feel better by talking to them and sharing his time. Prior to his illness Dean's idea of helping someone was to throw money at the problem. When he did talk to people he would always talk about himself or his own interests, like golf or cars. Now he was different. He was genuinely interested in hearing other people's stories and had a humility and empathy for people in difficult situations that I'd never seen in him before.

There was no one more surprised than me when Dean suggested going to day care at St Leonard's Hospice. The old Dean would have been very critical of anyone going to any type of day care and it certainly wouldn't have been anything he would have got involved in. Yet, here he was, compiling quizzes and buying games, like bingo and Snakes and Ladders, for people to join in. 'I want everyone to come together so that we can get to know each other,' he said. I began to see the comfort he was getting from becoming social. He had an overwhelming feeling of love that shone through everything he did and it was a joy to see.

'I have no fear, Joanne,' he said. 'I'm no longer frightened of leaving or the dying process.' When that time came for Dean, I felt loneliness like I'd never known. I never realised you could be surrounded by people and yet feel so alone. It was as if we were two pieces of a jigsaw and I'd lost the part that made me complete.

I thought about Dean and the faith that had transformed him in those last months. He would say, 'Yes, I've lost a lot, but I've gained so much more', and he meant it. He believed that he was going on to greater things, and while I was sad to see him go, I felt there was something wonderful waiting for him and that gave me hope that there was good waiting for me too. If asked, I always said I was a Christian, but after watching Dean I realised that my whole life, I'd been paying lip service to a faith that I thought I had. Now I wanted a real belief. I wanted to feel what it meant to be a Christian in the way that Dean had felt it. If he could get through everything he did and cope so well, then I could get through my loss, by finding my own relationship with God.

I took the opportunity to join an Alpha course at the church I'd first started attending with Dean. For me it was a fantastic opportunity to debate ideas and ask the questions that had been burning in my heart. About five weeks into the course we started to talk about the Holy Spirit. I'd always believed that the Holy Spirit was there for people in certain positions, like the clergy. I didn't realise that the Holy Spirit was there for me too and all I had to do was ask. Once I grasped that, my own relationship with God started to grow. God was no longer this idea in my head of an elderly gentleman sat on a cloud. I knew God was with me at all times, without question, and it was as if every light in the world had gone on. It was like a new life was starting, new opportunities were opening up for me, and I felt that things would get better.

My life is very different now. It might sound corny to say that when I wake up in the morning everything seems a little bit brighter, the sky looks a little bit bluer and life seems to have more perspective, but it is true. I am more open-minded and with that has come a softness of heart that has enabled me to become more easily involved with a whole range of different people. I see positive things in people and in situations that previously would've passed me by, and I don't take little things for granted that I once might have dismissed as unimportant.

I didn't expect that I would be a widow at 50, but that is how things have turned out for me. I realise that there are a lot of things in life that we have no control over, and I'm happy not to have control. I don't feel a compulsion anymore to live my life by a certain structure and order, and with that change has come a freedom to enjoy my life. When I wake up in the morning, whatever opportunity comes my way I take it in the surety that God is guiding me. I don't need to know his plan in advance. All I need to know is that he will bring to me the things I need at different times in my life. So many doors have opened and I'm sure there are more opportunities to come. I never would have thought I'd be actively involved in my community and have such a diverse life in the church.

Doing the Alpha course was a wonderful experience for me, and now I'm helping to run a similar course. I learned from Dean in his final months that it is so important for me to use whatever abilities and opportunities I have to help other people. I get involved in as many things as I possibly can because I realise that to be able to give is a gift in itself. The change in me has been amazing. My outlook feels brighter and more energised, so much so that if you could plug me into the mains I think I could sustain the whole of Yorkshire! I want to do so many things that at times I need to rein myself in. From being in a place of no hope, I'm now excited about what the future will bring, and for that I thank God every day.

11 'Families are made in heaven and on earth'

Rachel Poulton

'Father of orphans and protector of widows, is God in his holy habitation. God gives the desolate a home to live in; he leads out the prisoners to prosperity' (Psalm 68:5 & 6a).

John Sentamu writes:

God's heart reaches out for the most vulnerable in our society. To be an orphan or to be widowed, when this psalm was written, meant having no means of protection and facing destitution. But God notices these people, and his desire is to look after those in need.

Friends, this is not some sort of disembodied hope – it takes people who share that heart of God to make that longing a reality.

In Rachel and Nigel's story we have an amazing tale of family, a family that is created by putting into practice the love of God. Rachel responds with God's heart to people without family. Did you know that in Yorkshire and Humberside there are currently 800 children who need fostering or adoption? The needs of those orphaned and those widowed are not confined to the past.

As a parent and foster parent of four children who have now grown up, I am aware of the joys and challenges involved. I am also the sixth of thirteen children, so you can imagine that our house was never quiet! But it was always the place where you knew you would find a welcome. Be inspired, Rachel's love-in-action story is remarkable!

✠

Rachel Poulton's story:

As a child my favourite toy was a set of nine Russian dolls that I would pretend were my little family. Looking back it was always my dream to have lots of children, but there was a point where a big family looked like the last thing I'd be able to have.

When I met my husband, Nigel, we were both 24 years old and doing relief work with Khmer Rouge refugees in Thailand. Through our work we had both witnessed great need, and although we didn't know each other very well when we decided to marry, we could see in each other a desire to help people and to serve God. After getting engaged I remember walking on the beach and talking about what our future might look like. We both shared a strong desire to have children and within that to welcome other children into our family.

At the time I was working as a children's nurse and had gone to Thailand to work with malnourished children on the country's border with Cambodia. When I arrived twenty children a day were dying, largely from preventable diseases. Many more babies and children were being abandoned, so we began running an indigenous fostering and adoption scheme in the refugee camp. It was humbling to see people who had lost everything being willing to take in another child, and as we talked, Nigel and I agreed that if it were possible, we would like to be able to open our home in the same way. In our mind it was like the lesson from the parable of the talents, that we should use what we've been given, and we had been given so much: we had enough food, we had a home, we had each other, we had our family, why couldn't we share a bit?

In our heads it was all mapped out – we would have a child in the UK and then we would go abroad and work for God. Life didn't happen that way. It was the 1980s and the culture at home was very much about getting ahead, buying a bigger house and going for what you want. It felt quite strange for us because we didn't want very much at all, not materially anyway. We wanted to work in relief and development overseas, and we wanted a baby.

For a while we were thinking, we're Christians, we want to work for God abroad, what's wrong? Why can't God just give us a child? Then about a year-and-a-half into our marriage a doctor told us that we couldn't have children. For us, the news was devastating. It felt like everything I'd ever dreamed of and everything we'd planned for our life together had been taken away.

We were fortunate that through the sadness we grew closer, protecting and supporting each other. It didn't happen immediately, but soon we realised that there was no point in asking why. Instead we needed to ask, what do we do now? What good can come out of this? I believe in miraculous healings, I've seen it happen and it's great, but it doesn't always happen. It was humbling to have to accept that we weren't always in charge of our lives, and to learn to be more open to God and accepting of what comes. I don't know why things happen, but I believe in a God who is completely just and loving. Even if we don't understand at all, the future might bring something different than we had planned and it might be better for us.

Before we got married, Nigel and I had always said that we'd come home for a while to get to know each other's families and then we'd go abroad again to work in crisis situations. Our desire to do that hadn't changed, although we knew if we were to go overseas that we couldn't begin the adoption process in the UK. Sadly, the two were not compatible. So followed four years of development work in Bangladesh, and it was there we met our twin daughters.

Nigel and I had both visited orphanages before and were aware that they are emotionally charged places. That, coupled with our longing to have children, meant that we knew our hearts would be pulled and we didn't want to make an emotional decision or to take the idea of adopting lightly in any way. We had thought it through thoroughly. All the children in the orphanage had suffered the pain of bereavement or separation from their birth parents and that loss needed to be acknowledged. Of course it would be best for children to grow up with their birth parents, the next best would maybe to have been adopted by a loving family in their country of origin, but for these tiny twins there was absolutely no chance of either of those scenarios happening. They were 16-months-old, rather malnourished and had been through a lot of illness. As soon as we saw them we knew they were the children we were going to adopt. Nine days later they came home to us, and a year-and-a-half after that we had adoption papers and passports for the girls.

I can still hear the judge's hammer banging on the table in the adoption court. In that moment it wasn't just the girls' nationality that changed; our whole family changed. We later adopted three more children in Uganda, Thailand and Cambodia. To the outside world we didn't look like a family, but families can be made in heaven and on earth, and to me, our growing family was God at work, putting people together who needed each other.

We came back to the UK as our children became teenagers. Prior to that we'd been living in a very remote part of Laos for four years, where we had to drive 250km just to make a phone call. It felt like the right time to come home because the children had GCSEs and university ahead of them, but it was quite an adjustment for all of us.

We tried to keep up some of the little things that we'd done in Laos, like chopping chips together on a Friday night and watching a film. We also had what we called special nights, because there are a lot of us. So, for each of the five children, from Monday to Friday one of them could stay up later than the others and have our undivided attention.

On our return, Nigel and I both studied for Masters degrees in social work and ended up working with children. We are incredibly fortunate in that we both have the same desire to help children and to welcome people into our home. If it was just one of us pushing the other, because we love each other one of us would probably tag along, but it's not like that. We enjoy seeing children's lives get better and it is something that completely unites us and that we love to do. The needs of children in the UK are different from those we had seen in refugee crisis situations, but we soon became aware that there are still many children in need of love and care.

There is a lot of hopelessness about, and you can begin to think that the situation for children without families abroad or in the UK is hopeless, but it isn't, not really. When we first came back to the UK we started doing short-term fostering for children with disabilities, then as our children became young adults we started to foster more children. All of our children sustained massive loss as infants and I'm grateful that they haven't grown up with a chip on their shoulder or feeling that it's blighted their life in some way. They are all really positive and I'm always amazed at how accepting and welcoming they are to others, especially to the other children who join our family. It has worked out well because the older ones love coming back to a lively home and younger ones like to see all these people in their twenties who are cool and understand all of the latest electronics.

We check with our children to ask if they are happy with more people joining the family, and they always give the same

answer, 'It's fine as long as you don't get too tired.' It is tiring
sometimes, of course. We've been punched, kicked, bitten,
and stolen from in our home. All those things come with
fostering because people have been hurt. Sometimes things
don't turn out as we'd like, but that's all part of it too because
once we commit to caring for a child it's not with the thought
that we'll do something and get a particular result – it's not
a formula. One little girl came to us and she'd been hurt so
badly, she couldn't have been hurt more really in any way.
After about a year she was at the piano and we discovered
she was quite musical, so we got her lessons and she started
making up her own songs – it's wonderful to see that kind of
healing.

I'm not always very good talking about my faith, but I hope
that through seeing our family and being in our home, people
will catch something of God's love. Meal times are special
for us. We always have breakfast and evening meal together.
It's a very simple routine, but often these are the things that
the children we foster have been missing. There are ten of
us in the family now, and we often have my mother, who is
88 years old, with us, and another dear friend who is 92. As
we sit down to eat we always light a candle. It softens the
light and somehow unites us around the meal table. For me
it is a reminder of our Saviour who brings light and hope to
the world and it makes me feel incredibly grateful. We talk
about the day and there is always a lot of laughter. Nigel has
a wonderful sense of fun which has fed through our family;
without him I would have been much more serious.

We have our ups and downs like any family, but people often
comment on how close we are and I'm pleasantly surprised
that even now, when our eldest girls are 27 and married, all
the children still love to come on our family holiday. Last year
12 of us went on holiday to Greece and the summer before
there were 16 of us. Basically, once someone is in our home we
count them as family, and everyone who is part of our family
at that point is invited on holiday with us. Sometimes I catch
people looking at us at the airport and trying to work out how

we all fit together. Seeing their puzzled looks always makes me smile. Our family includes people from nine ethnicities, people with physical disabilities and people with learning disabilities. In one way we don't look like a family, but we are.

I often think of Psalm 68, God places the lonely in families, because it speaks to me about our life. The last thing I expected to be doing at 55 years old was looking after more children, and it's amazing to think that at my age our family is still changing and growing. We're not bringing more children into our home because we think we should, it's just something that we delight in doing. It is beautiful to see someone's life turn around and it is a huge privilege to be even a small part of that. I never imagined that my life would turn out this way, it's been a surprising journey that is still unfolding.

12 'A second chance'

Andrew Hall

Job said: 'Naked I came from my mother's womb, and naked I shall return there; the Lord gave and the Lord had taken away; blessed be the name of the Lord' (Job 1:21).

John Sentamu writes:

I don't know if you have read the Book of Job? Job was a good and a patient man. He trusted and he praised God. But he had a terrible time!

Father Andrew Hall in this next chapter tells us of his troubles too and of his trust in God in testing times. He explains how God protected and provided him with a new path to follow.

Like Job, whenever we experience tough times, we can still trust in God to get us through. The valley of the shadow of death may feel very real at times.

You might recall the *Footprints in the Sand* poem by Margaret Powers? At the last scene, a man looks back on the footprints in the sand to find that at the lowest ebbs, in the most troublesome parts of his life, there was only one set of footprints there. He did not understand why the Lord would leave when he needed him the most. The Lord replied: *'When you saw only one set of footprints, it was then that I carried you.'* In the storms of life, Jesus Christ is with us.

☩

Andrew Hall's story:

Every day people walk out of hospital after hearing news that has turned their world upside down. I'd probably walked past several of them on my way to the car park, but I wouldn't know, just as they didn't know what I had been told.

'We've no silver bullet,' the consultant said. As I heard those words, everything changed for me, yet there I was standing at the pelican crossing and it was as if nothing had changed. The world was going on as normal, but it felt like someone had pressed pause on my life. I wanted to shout out, 'My world has stopped. I'm going to die.' I didn't, of course. I simply made my way home silently, with the consultant's words ringing in my ears.

I knew that I wasn't well, but it took a year of investigations to find out what was troubling me. You see, to the doctors, I didn't look like a typical patient with hepatitis C.

Hepatitis C is a virus that infects the liver, and it had been silently attacking mine for the past 20 years without me knowing a thing about it. The virus is transmitted when blood from an infected person gets into the bloodstream of another. In the UK, 90% of cases are caused by sharing needles to inject illegal drugs. When I first started with symptoms I was 35 years old, I was married to a wonderful woman and we had two beautiful young children. I was working as an engineer, and held respected positions in the community as an elder in the church, and a school governor. My past was firmly in my past, so no one thought to ask me, 'Have you ever injected drugs?'

It wasn't that I was hiding anything, but the teenager who injected drugs was so far removed from who I had become that I never thought to mention it. I had changed and I rarely thought about those days any more. When I became a Christian the whole message was about Jesus forgiving my sins and making me pure. I had believed this and my life was transformed, so to learn that my blood wasn't clean, that I'd been walking around with what felt like the plague for years, made me feel cheated.

One of my reports from High School read, 'Andrew is of above average intelligence, but is easily led and distracted by others.' How true that was to become for too many years. I left school at 16 with no qualifications to speak of and took an apprenticeship in the mining industry. It was a good opportunity, but I found no satisfaction in my work, it simply provided the money for me to escape in music and illegal drugs with the friends I thought of as my brothers and sisters of soul. We travelled up and down the country to different club venues, and for a time it felt exhilarating.

It was into this world that my girlfriend and I had our first baby. To get married in the Church of England we needed to go to church three times to hear our banns read out, announcing our intention to marry. At first I went because we had to, but after the three obligatory services I wanted to keep going. For one hour in the week my life felt different and in the other people at church I saw the possibility of a different lifestyle.

At that time some of the people I was knocking around with had died of drug overdoses, one of my best friends had died on a scooter rally and another had shot himself. I didn't know what had gotten hold of us, but there had to be something better than this and I prayed for God to help us find it.

One day while I was praying in church, I felt something which was more than I could make up and bigger than the rush of any drug. I'd experienced the highs and lows of heroin, morphine, amphetamines and cocaine, but this was something completely different. I couldn't explain it. I wasn't taking any drugs but I felt better than I'd ever done.

From that night my life slowly began to change for the better. I found the strength to stop using drugs and regained everything I'd thrown away. I went to college and gained Chartered Engineering status, I applied myself to my job to gain a Colliery Manager's certificate, which was quite an achievement for an easily led, Yorkshire lad. God had redeemed me then and I'd worked with him every step of the way, so how could I turn my back on him now?

That's what I told myself, but when I cried out to God the silence was devastating.

More tests over the next couple of weeks revealed that my liver damage was such that I could only survive for two to five years. Having a successful liver transplant was my only hope for survival, but the idea of it brought up so many emotions. The idea of organ donation, of something good coming out of death, sounded all well and good when it was happening to someone else. Now it was me, I didn't know what to think.

I was given a pager and told that when it beeped I was to phone the hospital and come in for a transplant. I never had to do that because my health deteriorated so rapidly that I was admitted.

My life depended completely on another person whose death would give me new life, and with that gift would be the inescapable sadness of a life, so full of potential being taken away. It was an uncomfortable thought, but I only had to look around me to see that life held no guarantees. There was no guarantee that a suitable donor would be found, or that if I was to get a transplant that it would be a success. I watched the porters come onto the ward with a black body bag, for the fourth or fifth time that night. The air was so heavy with death it was like I could almost touch it. 'Please, Lord, I don't want to leave this ward in one of those body bags,' I prayed. I put my headphones on and started singing along softly to the music. My body was so full of toxins that I felt in another world. Then, I felt a calm peace fill my body. I wasn't trying to be all religious, but I sensed that God was telling me that it wasn't my time, that he still had work for me to do here.

Although my body was filled with toxins and I was in another world, I felt like God had given me something to hold on to. He had given me a message and I was going to get through this ordeal.

When the first liver became available I was all excited. I signed the consent form and was ready to go into surgery, but when the time came for the operation I sensed that something was wrong. 'Look, you'll have to tell him,' I heard one of the nurses say, as if they were drawing straws to decide who was going to deliver the bad news. The doctors had decided that I wasn't well enough to survive the operation. Instead another man came in. He had been hiking in the hills when his bleep went off. He was in and out of the hospital in eight days. I'd already been there three months.

'What's happened there, Lord?'

Eventually the medical staff stabilised me and I was prepared for the operation again, only to find that this time when they went to retrieve the liver it was too damaged. It was rare for this to happen and I thought that I must have got it wrong, perhaps it was my time to go after all? I began to doubt that God had something better for me, but at the same time something in me still believed in what I'd heard, after all what else did I have to hold onto if not my faith? I asked my wife to place her hands on my chest and pray that the seed of doubt that had rooted itself there would be shifted. In April, four months after I'd been admitted to hospital, the wait was over – a suitable liver became available and my operation was a success.

Although I had a new liver the virus was still in my body. The prognosis at the time was that I'd need another transplant every five to seven years. I was asked if I would like to join a clinical trial, which involved taking a combination therapy of drugs to help kill the virus. It was explained to me that the trial had a 33% chance of working, and they were looking to see if it would be better than another transplant. 'If you decide to go ahead it would only be 48 treatments,' the doctor told me. It didn't sound like many, but it would mean taking the treatment for almost a year with no guarantee of success.

While on the trial I was given a series of injections every Friday evening, and then I had to inject myself every other day with different drugs.

I'd prolong taking the injection by inviting friends to our house on Friday for a meal. I knew once I took the treatment I would be ill and the weekend would disappear in a blur of vomiting and trembling. Usually I'd feel unwell until Wednesday and then Friday would come round and the cycle would start all over again.

Over the 12 months we built up some wonderful relationships with the specialist nurses and the consultants. We were on this journey together. It was a new treatment and the medical staff were emailing their colleagues all around the world about what they were doing. They very much wanted it to work but none of us knew what to expect.

For me, I'd already come through a massive ordeal. When it came to checking my viral load I realised that my journey was no longer about simply clearing the virus, rather it was about how much I trusted God. Could I still trust him when the statistics weren't pointing in my favour? Could I still trust him if the treatment didn't work?

I'd been reading the book of Job because for me it's a book about faith. When Job said, 'Although He slay me, yet will I trust Him', I realised that was how I felt – my hope in God was no longer reliant upon receiving a physical healing.

I was the first person in the UK to clear the hepatitis C virus after a liver transplant using this treatment. All the staff were excited to tell me the good news. 'Andrew we couldn't have done it if it weren't for your determination and your belief in us,' the consultant said. 'You've given us the inspiration to carry on.'

When the consultant first suggested the trial I had thought, this is not the road I want to travel, I've already had enough.

Now I was being told that I was clear and because of me the doctors now had the confidence and the statistics to roll out the treatment to other people so that they might be cleared of the virus too. It was amazing.

It's 14 years since I had my liver transplant and 10 years since I cleared the virus from my blood. The treatment I trialled has since developed and now has a higher rate of success. There is a phrase, 'born again'. Well it is almost like I've been born again, for a second time, but this time there is a physicality to it as well as a spirituality. I've been given an organ, but it is so much more than that. It's an incredible gift, which has given me a real joy for life. I've been given a second chance and I want to do and be the best I can.

13   'Knowing I'm not alone'

Patricia McCaffry

Jesus said, 'I am with you always' (Matthew 28:20).

John Sentamu writes:

'A place for everything, and everything in its place' - or so the saying goes. And all too often in today's society, the place for anything that might look like 'religion' is in private or in Church. On a Sunday. For an hour. But no more.

We can start to believe that God isn't interested in the rest of our lives, or that God can't do anything during the other 167 hours in our week. And yet the promise of Jesus Christ is that He is with us always. Not just in the good times when we might be feeling 'religious'. Not just in the bad times when we find ourselves crying out to God in desperation just to see if He is there, pleading for Him to make a difference.

But Jesus Christ with us at all times. *'For better, for worse. For richer, for poorer. In sickness and in health.'*

It is this experience of the extra-ordinary God in the midst of ordinary life that has transformed ordinary life into something extra-ordinary for so many people, including Patricia.

God is not just the God of the hour in church on a Sunday. God is the 24/7 God who longs for us to know Him in who we are and in everything that we do. He longs for us to be filled with the Holy Spirit in every moment of our lives, so that we can be part of the adventure that is life with God 24/7.

✟

Patricia McCaffry's story:

Sometimes it's not easy to pin-point when problems start. That was certainly true in my case. I had got myself into a muddle with money, but because I didn't know how I'd got into it, I didn't know where to start to get out of it. In hindsight, you might say that I was a spendthrift. I didn't particularly have a lot to show for it, but I would buy anything that caught my eye, regardless of whether or not I needed it.

When I first moved to Newcastle-upon-Tyne I felt like I had a lot of money, so my spending didn't matter. Then my income was cut and soon the bills started piling up. After a while I didn't even open the letters anymore, I just put them in a drawer and forgot about them. Except I couldn't really forget about them because there would be another bill to follow, and then another, and then a threat of court action and bailiffs, until I was afraid to answer the phone or open the door in case it was someone asking for money I didn't have. I walked my Jack Russell dog, Louis, at strange hours when I hoped that no one would see me. I didn't speak to anyone and if anyone spoke to me I told them in no uncertain terms to leave me alone.

Eventually I told the warden at the housing association that I was in debt and she gave me a phone number for Christians

Against Poverty (CAP). 'I don't know much about them, but I've heard they do good things,' she said. I dialled the number she gave me. I didn't hold out much hope for a response, but I knew deep down that I needed help, although what help and how that help would come, I didn't know.

Not long after the first phone call to CAP a woman called Gwyneth came to my flat. She brought paperwork about the organisation and a DVD for me to watch. I sat there as if I was listening, but what she was saying to me just went in one ear and out the other. Then, before she left Gwyneth asked, 'Can I pray with you?'

'Please yourself,' I said. My tone was clipped and aggressive, although my animosity wasn't aimed particularly at Gwyneth, it was how I was with everyone at that time. Whatever Gwyneth said to me I came back with a negative response, so when she left I didn't expect to see her again. I expected her to be frightened off and leave me alone, just like everyone else.

I wasn't always an angry person. When I was younger you might have described me as bubbly. I worked as a nurse in a hospital for a long time and was very outgoing when my three children were growing up. I don't know where all the anger came from, again I don't think it came out of any one thing.

As with anyone, I'd had my ups and downs. I split from my husband but we remained best friends until he died suddenly of a heart attack when he was thirty-eight. I remarried, but it was too soon for me and it didn't last. I've had health problems for a long time. When I was thirty-one years old I went into hospital for a general hysterectomy. During surgery the doctors found that I had bowel cancer and it was another 15 months before I got home. I still have chemotherapy and radiotherapy treatment for that now, thirty-two years later. Although the treatment makes me tired I've always coped well on my own, but when I had a stroke a few years ago, my son suggested that I move from my home in Devon to Newcastle, to be closer to him. He found me a flat in sheltered accommodation and I agreed, although the move was quite an upheaval. I had two dogs, Louis and his twin sister, but there wasn't enough room in my new flat for me to bring both of them.

I'd never lived anywhere as small as the flat I moved into and I cried every day for six months because I disliked it so much. From then on it felt like one thing after another was going wrong. My income was cut, I didn't have any friends, and I didn't want to make any either. I wasn't nice to anyone, not even myself. I'd stay in bed all day, although I didn't sleep. I stopped eating properly, and I was probably on the verge of taking my own life when I met Gwyneth, who despite my best efforts to put her off did come back. This woman is stubborn like me, I thought, she's not going to give up. I decided to give her a chance, after all things couldn't get any worse.

It turned out that I was about £5000 in debt, which to me was a tremendous amount. To start paying it back, Gwyneth helped me to work out a budget that I could live on. I agreed to pay an amount of money into a CAP account each month and that money was used to pay off my debt. It meant that CAP stood between me and my creditors, so I didn't have to deal with them. I was a bit nervous about the process at first but if I was worried about anything I could ring Gwyneth and she'd talk to me or she'd say, 'I'm driving past your way, I'll nip in to see you', or 'I'm in such and such a day, we'll sort it out then', and I learned to trust her, because it always did get sorted out.

Gwyneth soon became much more to me than someone who sorted out my finances; she was a friend. Every time she visited she prayed with me, and after a while I didn't mind at all, in fact I quite liked it, so I asked about her church and she invited me to go along.

Gwyneth went to a community church that was held in a school hall, which I didn't recognise as a church in any way.

'That's it. I've tried it now, never again,' I told her. 'When that fog horn started up, it was just horrible.'

'You mean the saxophone?' Gwyneth asked.

That was what I meant, but to me it might as well have been a fog horn. I couldn't cope with noise of any kind. The saxophone overshadowed everything and was my reason not to go again. Gwyneth didn't try to change my mind. She continued to support me with regular visits and once I'd been paying in to my CAP account for four months the charity treated me to a four day break at a spa hotel.

'Are you excited about it?' Gwyneth asked.

'Not really,' I said, and it was true, I wasn't.

I travelled in a minibus with other people who had been supported by CAP for about the same length of time as me, and, although I hadn't been looking forward to the break, it felt good to be looked after. We had our meals cooked, we went on a trip to a park, we were pampered with massages and face creams and nail polish, and there was something comforting about being with other people who were in the same boat as me. I didn't feel so alone. We were from all different walks of life, but we all had one thing in common, we all had money worries.

When I got home I asked Gwyneth if I could go to church with her again. 'Make me go,' I said, 'It'll make me feel better.' I still hated the saxophone, but after a few weeks even that didn't seem so bad. Through Gwyneth I got to know some other people in the church and a couple of months later I was invited to go on a weekend away to Scarborough.

'I can't afford that,' I told Gwyneth.

'But would you like to go?' she asked. It came as a surprise, even to myself, to realise that I wasn't making money an excuse. If I had the money, I would like to go.

I couldn't afford it, of course, while I was paying off my debts, but to my surprise the church offered to pay for me to go and I went, gladly. We travelled to Scarborough on a Friday and came back on a Sunday. The group was all people I had met at church. We prayed together, we sang together, we had coffee together, we had our meals together – we were like one big family. It was completely spiritual and something I'd not known in my life. At the Sunday service everyone was singing wholeheartedly, I saw how everyone praised God for the good in their lives and it was overwhelming. I started to cry because I grasped what it was all about – God is there for me, for all of us, 24/7. Whoever we are, whether we're good or bad, he's there for us. There's no going back now, I thought. There's no turning around, if I want to enjoy my life, I've got to go forward.

When I picked Louis up after the weekend, he raced to see me. It brought tears to my eyes because I was so pleased to see him. I really had missed him and I realised that I hadn't just been neglecting myself, I had neglected him too. Not on purpose. At the time I didn't want anything in my life and, although I would never hurt Louis, I realised that he had been pushed out, that it wasn't just me who was suffering, it was the little dog too.

After that I did feel different. I can't say how or why, but something had changed. I realised that I had to do something and that I could do something to change my life. I began praying a lot, but it felt more like an on-going conversation with God. I'd be standing at the kitchen window and I'd talk to him, I'd be walking round the lake and I'd talk to him, or I'd be lying in bed and I'd be talking to him. Life started to even out for me. I didn't seem so worried, and I wasn't as agitated. Every now and then I'd get a glimpse of peace, a realisation that I might feel low now, but I'd be back to normal soon. I started walking Louis more and noticing things around me like the trees and the bird song. I began talking to people in the complex where I live and made some friends.

It took me just over two years to pay off my debt, but I did pay it off and everyone got their money back. I still live on the small budget that Gwyneth helped me put together and the money I used to pay to CAP goes into a savings account. It means that I've probably got more money now than I've ever had. I've learned a hard lesson and I don't spend money that I haven't got, but I know that if I stick to my budget, every so often I will have saved enough money to do something special.

I don't worry about money in the same way. I feel more in control of what I'm spending, and I enjoy what I do buy. Little things, like treating a friend to lunch, I would never have felt able to do. Knowing I'm not alone, that I have God with me 24/7 has changed my outlook. I've started enjoying my life and where I live. I've made friends in the complex. We meet in each other's homes – we chat, we laugh and it's nice. They understand if I need some time by myself because I'm feeling unwell after my treatment and need some peace and quiet on my own. I've started to enjoy living in the flat. Recently I bought some paper and paint to freshen up the bathroom. Every time I go in, I think how nice it is. I couldn't have done that a few years ago.

In a few months I am flying to Canada for my granddaughter's wedding. It was so lovely to be able to go to the bank and know that I had enough money to withdraw the cash for the ticket. I could never have imagined doing that before. In the last few years my life has completely turned round for the better – I think I've surprised everyone.

14 'A father to the fatherless'

Ian Williamson

Zacchaeus stood there and said to the Lord, 'Look, half of my possessions, Lord, I will give to the poor; and if I have defrauded anyone of anything, I will pay back four times as much.' Then Jesus said to him, 'Today salvation has come to this house, because he too is a son of Abraham. For the Son of Man came to seek out and to save the lost' (Luke 19:8-10).

John Sentamu writes:

Jesus always surprised his followers with his choice of those he wanted to spend time with. When Jesus arrived in the town of Jericho, he didn't choose to eat with the religious types but invited himself to stay for a day at the home of a despised tax collector who cheated people out of their hard-earned cash. For Zacchaeus this encounter was life-changing.

Ian, at first glance, might have looked the least likely person that Jesus might have wanted to spend time with! In fact, Ian went out of his way not to have an encounter with Jesus, but Jesus wasn't going to give up.

Like Zacchaeus, Ian's life was completely turned around and he was quite literally given a new lease of 'life in all its fullness'. Inspired by a Psalm, Ian set up the charity SixtyEightFive in his beloved South Bank, an area he knows so well. Verses five and six of Psalm sixty-eight, speak of God as, *'Father of orphans and champion of widows, who restores the lonely to their homes; and leads out the prisoners, safe and sound.'*

In people like Zacchaeus and Ian we are reminded there is always a way back to God, and God's way is the way of life, trust and hope. It is the way home with God.

✠

Ian Williamson's story:

When I was eight years old my dad walked out one day and never came back. I didn't understand the reasons why, all I knew was that my dad didn't live with us anymore and we had to move house. Overnight we went from living in a nice house in a good part of town, to living on one of the country's toughest council estates in the South Bank area of Middlesbrough.

Suddenly my life was very different, and nothing I could do would change things back to how they were. I didn't fit in and the other kids' taunts only emphasised what I already felt. All I wanted was for people to like me. Once I became part of the drug scene I found what I thought were friendships initially, but they weren't really, it was just a masquerade. People used me and I used other people. Cocaine was my friend. Together we were invincible. I loved it and I wanted it, nothing else mattered.

By the time I was in my twenties I was spending about £500 a week on cocaine and I was probably using more than I was buying. I'd taken a job working as a nightclub doorman. In many ways it was the worst environment for me given my situation, but at the time it felt very beneficial. Not only was the work a source of income but I got to keep any drugs I confiscated. Well, that wasn't official, but I saw it as a perk of the job, and it helped to feed my addiction.

By this time I was well known in the area, and well liked, which meant that I could get my drugs upfront and pay at the end of the month. I didn't always know where the money would come from, but finding enough to pay the bill soon became a bigger high than the drug itself. It became like a hunt, a crazy game in which the consequences of losing were so heavy that the relief of winning was incredible. I'd have a few hours to find the money and in that time would go from being skint to having a few hundred pounds in my hand to settle the bill and a couple of hundred extra to buy some more drugs.

To win the game I ripped off a lot of people. If I knew a girl was interested in me I'd tell her I was skint and persuade her to take out a credit card for me. Once I'd reached the credit limit on that card I'd find another girl who could get a credit card out with a higher limit. I found a loop-hole which allowed me to rack up my own credit card debts to almost ten times my original limit. I told myself that if the bank was willing to loan me increasing amounts of money, it was just as greedy as I was.

I convinced myself that I wasn't doing anything wrong because I wasn't robbing old ladies or beating people up for the money. I justified my fraud, because nobody was getting physically hurt, even though what I was doing was illegal and ultimately somebody would pay for it.

I made a lot of excuses at that time. Whatever I did, there was always someone else to blame. One minute I'd be speaking to someone and the next minute they'd have a bleeding nose. It must have been their fault. If they hadn't looked at me the wrong way or said the wrong thing then I wouldn't have hit them. That's how I thought, and I know now that it was a horrible way to live.

Deep down I think I knew it then too, I just didn't know what to do about it. For a short time cocaine had given me the identity I was craving for. It made me feel secure, while masking the pain, fear and rejection that I didn't know how to deal with. For a long time I ignored the negative side of the drug – the sleepless nights, the paranoia, and how one minute I could be the life and soul of the party and the next, the most aggressive man in the room.

I hated myself, so much so, that one day I took a knife out in front of my mum and threatened to end my life. As I broke down in tears my mum held me and told me that Jesus could help me. It wasn't what I wanted to hear. At first I was angry, but my mum kept pleading with me to ask for help. I realised that I didn't have any answers myself so I did. 'I hate myself,' I cried, 'I hate who I've become, I hate my life. I want to change and I know I can't do it on my own. If you're there, God, please help me and I'll follow you'.'

The next day I woke up feeling so normal, that it was miraculous. Just to wake up in the morning look out of the window and notice the sky and the trees – things that most people see every day, but my life was so chaotic that I'd missed all this beauty around me. I remember walking through South Bank and waving to everyone. I felt fantastic, but after about three days I realised that, while I might have wanted my healing to be instantaneous, there wasn't going to be a quick fix.

When things went wrong I found it all too easy to fall back into my old ways. Working on the doors wasn't helping so I began to look for other work and eventually found a job with a charity based at the Baptist Church I used to go to as a kid, with my mum. As a teenager I'd felt that no one in the church understood me. I was a white working class male in a middle class church, and in my mind it was just one more place where I didn't fit in. I didn't have a problem with God or

Jesus, I had a problem with other Christians. I thought they were hypocrites. In my eyes, I was the only one who deserved grace or mercy and everyone else should be perfect. I heard the gospel, but I didn't understand it. I thought of Jesus as a fairy godmother who came to take away all my problems, rather than as someone who came to take away my sins. I saw myself as the victim and thought that Jesus should come to me because I deserved help rather than because I was a sinner and I needed forgiveness.

I don't think my views had changed much since then. To the other people in the church I probably came across as intimidating and aggressive, although I never saw myself that way. The problem was always with someone else. Then one day I recognised a woman in church who I used to buy drugs from when I was younger. She told me she had recently become a Christian and shared her story. As she talked I could relate to everything she said. It was so overwhelming that tears began to stream down my face. 'I'm tired', I said, 'I've had enough but I'm not willing to give up my life to follow God'. I didn't wait to hear her reply, by now I was weeping uncontrollably and left embarrassed.

A couple of weeks later I drew the short straw at work and had to go along to a Mother's Union carol service. I wasn't keen to go, but once there I enjoyed the peace that came with sitting in a big, old, brick building with nothing to do but rest and be still. I started thinking over the past few months. 'Okay, God,' I prayed, 'let me get Christmas out of the way and I'll get back to you in January.'

Obviously, I didn't want to give my life to God before Christmas, and miss the fun of the party season. As it turned out, that Christmas and New Year were among the worst of my life. I split up with my girlfriend and I had to move back in with my mum. To make some extra money I took work as a doorman, but I found the violence depressing. Everything seemed to be falling apart but this time, instead of blaming everyone else, I realised that I had to start taking some responsibility for the mess I was in. I'd carried a huge chip on my shoulder and felt sorry for myself for too long. I expected other people to have patience and grace with me, when I didn't have patience and grace with anyone else. As much as I played the part well, I realised that I wasn't really a victim, and I couldn't keep using what happened to me when I was eight years old as an excuse for how I was behaving at 28.

I explained how I felt to some men at church and they offered to help me. They said that I needed to move away from Middlesbrough because it held too many temptations for me. I knew that running away wasn't going to solve any of my problems because I'd moved to London once before, hoping for a new start, only to find that my problems followed me and became even worse. The men didn't mean for me to go that far. I still needed support of people I knew, and a few miles was far enough away to give me a chance to make a clean break. So, I moved to a small village called, Eaglescliffe, about eight miles away. Two men from the church helped me to get a flat and, while I started to make a new life for myself, they more or less babysat me. They'd turn up at my door first thing in the morning and last thing at night. They said they were coming to pray with me, but I knew they were really keeping an eye to see if I'd slipped back into my old ways. At times I found the visits a real pain, but a lot of the time, just them being there would diffuse my temptation before I got to the point of doing anything. They gave me a way out. Their being there meant that I couldn't use boredom as an excuse. When they weren't there, they had me involved in volunteer work when I wasn't working on my paid job. I never had a minute spare.

It was probably three years before I was completely clean and could say I had beaten the addiction, but during that time those men showed me a different way to be. I grew up not knowing how to be a man. My heroes were men who were physically strong, like Mike Tyson, Rambo and the local drug dealers. Seeing men who were strong emotionally and spiritually, and who could stand up to their responsibilities was new to me. I'd seen so-called hard men go to bed with swords or guns under their bed because they were petrified. The more they strove for security through muscles and weapons the more insecure they became. In contrast these men didn't have big muscles or weapons but they slept soundly at night. Jesus was their security, and seeing that lived out made me think, 'Wow, I want some of that.'

The peace they had fascinated me – these guys had never had a fight in their life yet they weren't frightened of anyone. I watched how they behaved as fathers. How they interacted with their children, the way they disciplined gently, how they reacted if their wives upset them and the other way around. It showed me a whole new way of being in a relationship and being part of a family.

Now I'm a father myself I'm even more aware of how many young people don't have positive male role models in their lives. I wanted to do something positive to reach working class men, like myself, who had grown up in a fatherless environment or who were fathers themselves. So, along with my wife, I set up the charity, SixtyEightFive and went back to South Bank to replicate in the community what the men at church had done for me. The name comes from Psalm 68:5 in the Bible about God being a father to the fatherless. I first heard it as a teenager when I went to the Lake District with a church group. All of us on the trip had one thing in common, we all grew up without a father, and that verse stayed with me, even through my wilderness years of taking drugs. Back then, I thought that cocaine held the answers for me, but it was like a buying a fake watch from a street seller – it looks great for a day but then your wrist turns green. I have no need for cocaine in my life anymore because I've been shown another way to live – I've found an identity with God that is priceless and eternal.

15   *'Spiritual spinach'*

Andy Roberts

'Whoever welcomes one such child in my name welcomes me. If any of you put a stumbling-block before one of these little ones who believe in me, it would be better for you if a great millstone were fastened around your neck and you were drowned in the depth of the sea' (Matthew 18:5-6).

John Sentamu writes:

In this uncompromising passage, Jesus speaks of God's will to protect the most vulnerable, the poorest, the defenceless, and those most likely to be overlooked.

Andy's righteous anger at the injustice and cruel abuse experienced in the lives of children in Orlinda, Brazil, led to the setting up of his charity, and the creation of a place offering care and protection for young girls caught up in prostitution.

Andy's story of hope is about recognising the deep love of God for his children, and responding with faith, determination and action. The Crucifixion of Jesus reminds us that there are no limits to how far God will go to right the wrongs of the world. For Andy, the streets of Brazil may seem a long way from his family home in York, but Jesus is willing to go further than any of us.

Andy's 'Popeye' response to the exploitation of the vulnerable reflects the righteous anger of Jesus Christ in the face of the pain and suffering of all God's children.

As we look at the news, should we ask the question whether we have lost our 'Popeye' response? Andy's story reminds us that, wherever we are, this is something we too can discover and act on every day.

Andy Roberts' story:

I first came to Brazil ten years ago as part of my gap year before going to university. I was on a mission trip, which I'd imagined would be like an extended holiday with an aspect of adventure. In my head, the trip was going to be something memorable that I'd do before I got on with the rest of my life, as it were. What happened next, I don't suppose anyone would have expected, least of all me.

I went to work on a project supporting boys living on the streets of Orlinda in North East Brazil. Orlinda is a place of huge contrasts. It is one of the best-preserved colonial cities in Brazil, which earned the downtown area UNESCO world heritage status in 1982. There is no escaping its beauty as you walk through the winding streets of old, colourful houses or visit one of its many Baroque churches. But there is another side to Orlinda, the favelas or slums, where houses aren't built of brick they're cobbled together with cardboard, metal sheets and anything that can be used to make a shelter. Beside those dwellings is an open rubbish dump on which people scrabble to find materials to build their homes, and sometimes for food. You see children literally eating rubbish. These children don't go to school, they wander the streets looking for any means to survive. That means that sometimes they steal, they sell drugs, they sell their bodies and they kill.

When I was a child I used to watch a cartoon called Popeye. Popeye was a sailor man and if anyone messed with his girlfriend, Olive Oyl you'd see the anger building up inside him until he couldn't take it anymore and he'd crack open a can of spinach, from which he'd gain all the strength he needed to sort out the situation, and save his girl. I thought about Popeye when I was in Brazil. The image kept coming to me as a wave of anger in a strange mix of remembering my own childhood and comparing it with the harsh reality of these street children. You can hear all of these stories and think how terrible they are, but it's hard to comprehend what it feels like to be approached on the street by a ten-year-old girl who is selling her body. The first time it happened to me, it broke my heart. That was my real Popeye moment, when I knew that I couldn't take it anymore. I didn't know what I could do about it, but like Popeye I knew that I had to do something. So, I suppose you might say that I turned to my 'spiritual spinach', to show me a way.

My answer didn't come immediately. After the six month placement I returned home to begin my degree as planned, but my heart stayed in Brazil in more ways than one. During that trip I met and fell in love with Rosie, who has since become my wife. I also couldn't stop thinking about the children I'd seen in the favelas. Knowing what I did about their abusive situations, how could I just walk away and leave them? Both ties on my heart raised questions about what I wanted to do with my life. Until then talking about the rest of my life had been hypothetical and had gone no further than me having some general thoughts about what I might like to do after my degree. Was my life about getting a good job to make as much money as I could, so that I could afford a good retirement home? There's nothing wrong with that, but thinking about life in that way made me think again about what the Bible has to say about our lives being fleeting. I suppose you could say that it made me live as if I really believed life was short. I started asking, what can I do with the years God has given me? How can I use them to have an eternal impact on this world? Am I going to treat Christianity like a spiritual hobby, or is it a way of life? I decided that after my degree I would go back to Orlinda and use the gifts and skills that God has given me to do whatever I could, and that is what I've done.

When I left the UK to work in Brazil full-time, I joined a project called, 'My Father's House', which provides a safe house, where young boys can escape from a life of crime and violence and begin to piece their lives back together. Through this work I was approached by a woman who asked if we could help her three nieces who were being sexually exploited. I met the sisters. They were aged eight, ten and 12, and all three were being sold on the streets of Orlinda as prostitutes. That in itself was hard enough to comprehend, and then I learned that the person selling these children was the one person who you would expect to love and protect them – their mother. These are the children that UNICEF refers to as 'invisible children'. The ones who are enduring systematic abuse in their homes and yet don't show up in the statistics so are not counted among the hundreds of thousands of child prostitutes on the streets of Brazil.

The 12-year-old told me that shortly before I met her she had been kidnapped by a client and spent two-weeks tied up in his room. I don't want to think about the kind of things that she went through during that time. She managed to escape and find her way home, only to be sold by her mother again, night after night, to whoever was willing to pay.

I wanted so much to help those sisters and I did try, but in the end I had to tell them there was nothing I could do. There were seven or eight charities that I knew of working in the city, but they were all working specifically with boys. For girls, there was nothing. As I told them I couldn't help, I felt the same Popeye moment as I had four years earlier start brewing inside of me. Such things shouldn't happen in a world like ours. I'm not talking about girls in their early twenties or even late teens working as prostitutes, these were children and they weren't alone. An investigation by the Brazilian government revealed that Orlinda is a hot spot for sex tourism. At one time Thailand was the place that paedophiles would flock to, but after the tsunami in 2004 destroyed many of those areas, for a time the sex trade moved to other shores. North East Brazil became the capital of the world for a certain kind of tourist who is coming for one thing, and that isn't to make the most of the beautiful beaches. When I read a statistic that the average age of a girl's first sexual encounter on the streets of Brazil is ten years old, I knew I had to crack open that spinach once again. My wife and I took the difficult decision to step back from our work at My Father's House, and started to look in to how we could set up an organisation to protect girls involved in sexual exploitation and prostitution.

We knew for the idea to work that we would need to have a property, so we started looking for a house to rent. It wasn't long before we found what we believed to be the perfect house to set up our new project we called, ReVive. There was one snag – the house was for sale, not for rent. However, through our enquiry we discovered that the house was owned by our daughter's doctor, who had recently moved into the apartment building where we lived. She was now living two apartments below us, which meant that we had the opportunity to chat with her and share our vision for ReVive. Once she knew our plans and how we aimed to restore these young lives and renew hope, the owner was keen for her house to be used in this way. She still needed to sell it, but she knocked a huge sum off the price. Unfortunately, even with the reduction and the funds we had, we were still £50,000 short of the asking price. On top of that, if we wanted the sale, we had to raise the money in three weeks.

Now, I don't know about you, but for us £50,000 is a lot of money. I didn't have it, and I didn't know anyone who did. I thought perhaps I could have raised it if I was given a couple of years, but three weeks – to do that would be nothing short of a miracle. For a long time one of my favourite Bible verses was from Philippians, 'Do not worry about anything, but in every situation, by prayer and petition, with thanksgiving, present your requests to God. And the peace of God, that passes all understanding, will guard your hearts and your minds in Christ Jesus.' For me, basically that passage is saying, what are you worrying about? Worrying isn't going to change anything. God has got it all under control; he made the world and he knows exactly what you need, so trust in him, tell him what you need and just chill out. In the work that we do in Brazil, you could say that we live by faith every day, so I realised that as much as I wanted it, I had to trust God in the same way with this project too. If it was his will then we had to believe that God would help us to find a way and it would happen.

We sent out a few emails to people who we knew were praying for us back in the UK, explaining our situation and asking if they would like to support us. Then we prayed about it and left the rest to God.

What happened next was amazing. People were so generous in their response. Within three weeks we'd not only raised the £50,000 to buy the house, but a further £10,000 to pay for the furniture and help with the ongoing running costs. It was a great answer to prayer, because with the help of God and all our supporters we'd done it – we'd opened the first project in Orlinda to work specifically with young girls involved in sexual exploitation. We'd created a safe house which can accommodate up to 12 girls living full-time. A place where girls can come to escape their abusive situation, to begin to learn skills that will help them to earn money in other ways, and to understand their true value as much more than any guy can pay for them.

We hope this house will be the first of many safe houses for girls on the streets of Brazil. So that, if I, or anyone else, meets children like those three sisters who inspired ReVive, we will be able to say, 'Life doesn't need to be like this and I know someone who can help you'.

16 'God as my anchor'

Luke Smith

Therefore do not worry, saying, 'What will we eat?' or 'What will we drink?' or 'What will we wear?' For it is the Gentiles who strive for all these things; and indeed your heavenly Father knows that you need all these things. But strive first for the kingdom of God and his righteousness, and all these things will be given to you as well. So do not worry about tomorrow, for tomorrow will bring worries of its own. Today's trouble is enough for today (Matthew 6:31-34).

John Sentamu writes:

This reading tells us today's trouble is enough for today. In Luke's story we find out that he has more than enough to worry about and he shows us that we cannot let fears crowd in and destroy us.

Luke's way of living is a rallying cry for us all to seek the Kingdom of God now. Don't put off the good you long to do now, hoping to find a better moment to do it. Tomorrow might be too late; in Jesus Christ, the time is always now.

I was inspired by Luke's words about living with love at the heart of everything. May we walk Christ every day. Live him every day. Know him every day.

✝

Luke Smith's story:

It can't be easy to know what to say to someone who has recently been told they've got a serious, possibly life-threatening illness. When I was diagnosed with bowel cancer just over a year ago, there was a lot of talk about positive thinking. Everywhere I went, I heard the same phrases: 'You've got to remain positive, that's the main thing.' 'As long as you keep positive, lad, you'll be fine.' 'You're right to be doing what you're doing, just keeping positive.'

The more people spoke to me about being positive the less motivated I felt to be positive. To me, their words were like seeing one of those badges that read, 'Keep smiling', which always made me want to do the opposite. I didn't want to criticise anyone, but these words felt vacuous. What did it mean, stay positive? To me, the idea of just staying positive, was like trying to keep my thumbs up and ignoring all the tough stuff, because if I was to look at that then I would become negative – and then what?

When I first became ill, I knew something wasn't quite right, but I didn't know what it was and neither did the doctors. I was constipated and as the month went on the problem got worse until the pain became so bad that I went to Accident and Emergency, and after a seven hour wait was admitted to hospital. A couple of days later I woke up after an operation to find that the surgeon had cut through my stomach muscles, removed a foot of my bowel, and given me a colostomy bag, which is where your bowel sticks out of your stomach. The following month I went back to see the consultant and he told me I had bowel cancer.

I was 33 years old and the doctor said that being young would help me recover from the surgery. 'That's good,' I thought, but then he said my age wasn't advantageous with regards to the disease. Cancer is based on cell multiplication and regeneration of mutated cells, so the younger you are the quicker your cells multiply, and the more serious it is if you get cancer – for me, that's not so good.

My prognosis is a complicated one. Bowel cancer is rare in a young person and the fact that I presented as an emergency doesn't do me any favours statistically. There is 40% chance that the cancer will come back again within five years. If I have chemotherapy, which I did, then that percentage falls by half, but nevertheless that's still a one-in-five chance, and I wouldn't take that on a Russian Roulette.

A one-in-five chance that the cancer will come back doesn't sound great, but a four-in-five chance of it not recurring sounds better. Both are true. No one knows what's going to happen. People can give me statistics, but that is only the collective data about other people. The statistics don't say anything about me as an individual. I might fall within the 20 per cent of people for whom the cancer returns, but I might not.

Being faced with such uncertainty made me reflect on everything – life and death, the tough stuff, the good stuff, friendships, what I truly value. I also had to think about what it means to be positive. For me, a positive thought is a good thought. A good thought process might involve facing the harsh reality full on, wading into fears and addressing them, looking at what lies behind them, bringing my true emotions to God and saying, please will you help me because this is too much for me to carry on my own.

When I was initially diagnosed, scripture became like bread and butter to me. I was so hungry for it. I was aware that what I was reading had been read by billions of people in the past, and for me, there was a reliability in that knowledge I could trust. There are loads of examples in the Bible of people going to God with their anger and frustration. Ultimately it led me to a place where I could say, I don't get this, God, but you probably do. I don't have the answers, I'm not in control and if I'm really honest, it's a good job I'm not in control because I wouldn't know what to do if I was. I'm glad that you are in control and I'm going to trust you through this next season because you're the shepherd and I'm the sheep. I realised that analogy is not used in the Bible by mistake. When we really need help, we need to follow someone the way a sheep follows a shepherd, because we haven't got a clue what's going on.

The Bible talks about walking through the valley of the shadow of death. It doesn't talk about going into the valley of the shadow of death, sitting down and getting depressed. It talks about going through it and having no fear because you know who your shepherd is, and trusting that he will lead you out the other side. In this way, for me, positive thinking wasn't about ignoring the bad stuff. It was more about finding hope bubbling out of something real, something that is deep rooted within me and also that is rooted in God. Yes, I've been angry and frustrated, but I feel like I've been able to cry all the tears I've needed to cry, which leaves me in a position where I am able to express true hope. Having gone through all the mess I've been able to come out of the other side and say, there is hope.

Although I've been a Christian most of my life and I'm also a church leader, none of this thinking came overnight. When I was in hospital it was so difficult to work out what was going on. I was just taking each minute as it came. Following my surgery I was in hospital for a week and then I came home, on bed rest, to recover. Aside from my illness there was a lot going on. We had just moved house. Aaron, our youngest son was three-months-old and Morgan our eldest, wasn't yet two. My wife, Hannah was downstairs looking after the boys and I was lying in bed thinking about how my life had changed in a week. I closed my eyes, but I couldn't stop tears from streaming down my face. I opened my eyes because I thought I felt someone sitting at the end of my bed, but no one was there. I can't explain it, other than it really did feel like someone was in the room with me, almost as if Jesus was sitting at the end of my bed. As I cried, I felt he was showing me the different places I'd been during the past seven days. We started with Saturday night in Accident and Emergency. There were a lot of drunk people in the hospital that night. The waiting room was noisy and felt chaotic. I was sitting on a stacker chair in easily the most pain I'd ever experienced in my life, and the loneliest I'd ever felt. As I lay thinking over this time, it was as if Jesus showed me a picture of himself sat next to me on a stacker chair, not saying anything, just being there with me. Then he took me through the different beds I'd been in, and each time he was there, sitting in a big chair next to my hospital bed. Even in the operating theatre Jesus was next to me. I could picture him, wearing a little face mask and cap like the surgeons wear. It was as though he was saying to me, 'I've been with you all the way. I'm still with you, and I'm always going to be with you', and, for the first time in a while, I felt peaceful. It's hard to put into words. People talk about the peace that surpasses understanding because we can't understand it. I can't explain it, but I know it's the peace of the Holy Spirit that allows me to say that no matter what happens, even if it's awful, I'm able to stay in hope because I trust God.

From the start my illness has felt like a journey. My situation isn't one that I would have chosen, but it feels like I'm going through a process from which I'll come out of the other side, although I don't know how. I knew that I had a hard year ahead of me, but I was determined not to come out of it bitter. I would seek God in all of the darkness and keep my arms reached out to him in whatever he was going to do. That didn't mean that I ignored the doctors, but nor did it mean that I lived under the authority of the statistics, which provide the evidence on which they base what they tell me about my condition. Instead I chose to live under the authority of what I know God has said about me and about all human beings. With God as my anchor I could go into the tough stuff and not get lost because I'm tethered to him like a climber would be secured by a belay. I'm roped on, so I can go into the dangerous place without getting lost.

I still get scared sometimes. I recently had a CT scan, which I will have every year now, where I go through a machine which looks like a big Polo mint, and my body is scanned for any tumours. Waiting for the results brought up my fears again. Not fears about what will happen to me if I die, but I do worry about leaving a young family behind. I don't think that thought will ever get easy, but then that's where I'm convinced I need to let uncertainty lead me to trust, rather than to fear. I don't think we can live without fear, but again it's whether we're able to face those fears, address them, and bring them to the foot of the cross and say to God, I don't want to carry these fears any more – I give them to you.

Almost a year after my initial diagnosis, I had an operation to reverse the colostomy and I'm now back together again. I feel in a privileged position coming into the new year. The practicalities of being ill, having chemotherapy treatment and not working, meant that I had to put down a whole load of things in my life and so did my wife, Hannah. Now we get to choose what we put back in, to piece our lives back together again from scratch.

There is something dynamic about living life fully in the knowledge that you don't know how long you've got left. The same is true for all of us, none of us knows when we're going to die, but we often live as if we assume death is going to be a long time in the future. My experience has made me think about how I would live differently if I knew that I might die soon. If I knew that I didn't have much time left on this earth then I would live today with more love, more generosity, more kindness, more forgiveness, more passion, more risk taking, and more grace for people than ever before. Then I thought, what is stopping me living that way now? The fact is, I might die young because I've got cancer, but I might die when I'm an old man – I don't know. If I live to be 85 years old having lived in the way I would do if I thought it might be sooner, I won't have lost anything. Living with love at the heart of everything I do, sounds a good way to have lived.

17 'My life mattered'

Shaun Turner

So Ananias went and entered the house. He laid his hands on Saul and said, 'Brother Saul, the Lord Jesus, who appeared to you on your way here, has sent me so that you may regain your sight and be filled with the Holy Spirit.' And immediately something like scales fell from his eyes, and his sight was restored. Then he got up and was baptized, and after taking some food, he regained his strength (Acts 9:17-19).

John Sentamu writes:

This reading from Acts, and Shaun's story, demonstrate that in a very real sense the future looks very different from the past. There is the possibility of hope even in our darkest moments.

Ananias took a courageous step forward in his decision to take a risk on someone who had a murderous reputation and intent. In reading Shaun's story, I was struck by individuals being agents of God's grace. Having that willingness to take the risk of responding in love to people the crowd would love to hate, and avoid. Our positive engagement of love creates that transformative response that follows.

Saul of Tarsus became Paul. Through a change of location and lifestyle, Shaun resolved that his life mattered. What was lost, he found. Like Saul, Shaun was encouraged by others who saw something within him that was worth holding on to, a person loved by Jesus Christ. In responding to that love made real by others, life would never be the same again.

✠

Shaun Turner's story:

I don't remember much about the first night I slept on the streets. At the time it was a choice I made. The idea of not caring about what anyone else thought or what I thought of anything was appealing to me. In this way, sleeping rough was a freedom that took away the pressures that had been building up in my life. I still miss that freedom sometimes, fleetingly – to be in my own little bubble and feel like I don't exist to the rest of the world.

In that sense it wasn't so much a choice to be homeless as to escape from my life as it was. Looking back, it wasn't such a terrible life but it wasn't a life that I wanted and I couldn't see how to change it. I can't say that there was one thing that happened to make me feel this way. I just found myself on a downward spiral and didn't know how to get out.

I was in my thirties when I became homeless. I can see now that I hadn't been coping very well for a few years before that, but no one who knew me would have guessed that I might become homeless. I'd had a very happy childhood and in many ways a very ordinary life.

I always worked and in my late twenties I had a responsible job as an area manager for a motor accessory company in Leighton Buzzard. I had been in the job for a few years but, as in lots of industries, things were changing and I became a bit disillusioned at work. My relationship broke down around the same time, so when the offer of voluntary redundancy came up I saw it as a chance to make a fresh start.

I decided to move back to Yorkshire where I grew up. The idea was to start again, but with some familiarity because I knew the area and my parents lived there. When I first moved back I spent a couple of months living with my parents but it didn't work out. My mum remarried, so the person I call dad now is my step-dad. It was the first time I'd ever really spent any time with them and I suppose that I was like a stranger in many ways. Growing up they were more like my aunt and uncle than my parents, because I was brought up by my grandparents.

Being raised by my grandparents was the only part of my upbringing that was unusual, but it wasn't something that ever worried me. It happened because my father had an affair while my mother was pregnant with me and he left her. When I was born my mum had to go to work, so my nan and granddad looked after me. They were looking after me most of the time and after a while I just never went home – it was as simple as that. It didn't feel unusual to me. As a child I was always happy and I knew that I was loved.

I don't know what I expected from moving back to Yorkshire, but it wasn't the new start I had hoped. I wasn't a child anymore and Yorkshire wasn't the same place I knew then. My grandparents had both died and I felt very lonely. Sometimes I wondered if I'd made a bad decision in putting myself forward for voluntary redundancy.

I'd felt redundancy was the right choice at the time and I did find another job quite quickly managing a warehouse, where I worked for three years. I rented a flat nearby, but life was lonely and I ended up drinking a lot when I was alone.

Early one morning I took the company van back to the warehouse and left the keys. I just wanted to get away, I didn't know where to. I took a taxi to Leeds station, a train to Manchester and ended up in Blackpool at eight o'clock in the morning. I remembered the beach from my childhood and had happy memories of family holidays there. I walked along the sea front, booked into a hotel, switched my phone off and spent a week drinking. When I eventually switched my phone back on I realised that the police had been looking for me because I'd been reported missing. It was clear that I wasn't coping very well and I spent a short time in hospital after that.

I went back to work for a while and my employer was happy to have me. I had spells, often months at a time, when I would pull myself together and become more focused, but it didn't take much for me to get upset and start drowning my sorrows in the bottom of a glass.

One day my employer spoke to me about drinking. He said, 'We can't have you driving the van when you're drunk. We'll talk about it next week.' I didn't want to talk about it. I wasn't drunk. He knew I'd been out the night before but I'd only been at a friend's house, we hadn't been drinking. I was drunk soon after we spoke. It was the first thing I did when I left work and I ended up being arrested for being drunk and disorderly. The next morning I was confused. I didn't lose my job, I just didn't go back.

I asked my dad to drive me to York. He pleaded with me to stay with him and mum for a while, but I didn't want to. Realising that my mind was made up, my dad drove me to York and helped me find somewhere to stay. I slept in a hotel that night, but the next night I slept rough.

There was something unreal about that first night I slept rough. I didn't need to do it because I still had money to pay for a hotel. I suppose it's like if you have to spend a night in an airport terminal, it's ok because you know that's not your life. In the same way I always had in the back of my mind that I could return to a warm house and sleep in a comfortable bed if I wanted to. I don't know how many weeks or months it was before it hit me that living on the streets was my life.

From that point everything becomes muddled. I can't put a time frame on when and where I was. I moved around so much. Survival was the most important thing. My issues became, where do I sleep, how much can I eat, am I too cold? I didn't care that I was unshaven and it became acceptable for me to walk around in the same set of clothes without having bathed or showered for a month.

I was never short of company. I soon found that people who are in the same situation tend to stick together, but they weren't forming friendships, it was people using each other as a crutch. After all it's better to spend time with a few others, even if it's just to relieve the boredom of having nothing to do. Life was the same every day and I couldn't see a way of changing that. On the streets alcohol became more important to me than food. I used it as another form of escape and the more I relied on it the more my life became a blur. I was regularly taken into custody for my own safety and the safety of others, and spent several spells in psychiatric hospitals. One day I stepped out in front of a bus on purpose and I don't remember anything after that until I woke up in intensive care four days later.

It wasn't the first time that I had tried to take my own life in this way. I know that there are far more efficient ways of doing it, but at the time I felt like I was putting my life in someone else's hands. For whatever reason I wasn't dead and I think that part of me subconsciously decided that I may have a future and so the help came along.

Once I recovered, I spent some time in a psychiatric hospital again, and this time when the section was lifted the mental health team found me a place to stay at a Salvation Army hostel in Bradford. People took time to spend with me, to listen to me and to take an interest in my life. It meant a lot, that I wasn't just a piece of paper being filed, but that I had an identity again.

When you are in the hostel system, you don't always have a choice about where you live. I hadn't been to Bradford before and I didn't want to stay there. I got a place at another Salvation Army hostel in Coventry. The building was old and if I stood up and opened my arms I could touch both walls of my room, but it didn't matter because the people were supportive and to me that was the most important thing. I started to see people regularly who could help me and not just once a week because I had to. I'd had so many disappointments in so many areas. To find that there were people out there who if I gave them a chance would give me a chance, made a huge difference to my outlook. They didn't give up on me, they didn't say your hour's up and we can't see you next week because we're busy. I respected them and because I respected them I listened to what they were saying. They saw something in me that was worth working for and gradually I began to believe it too.

I began to feel that my life was coming back, that life did matter, that my life mattered and what I did with my life mattered. I wasn't going to spend the rest of my life as an alcoholic with no home and no future. There was something better for me.

After a time I was fortunate to be offered a place at the Arc Light hostel and so I came back to York. I began to find that given the right help, I could settle, I could focus and I could have stability in my life. There were times when I would have re-lapses, I'd drink and I'd doubt if I was getting anywhere in life, but the staff encouraged me. Even when I had setbacks they still supported me. They told me that they could see something in me that could get through this time and make things better. That gave me a huge lift.

I hadn't touched alcohol for the best part of a year when I left Arc Light. In any hostel there comes a time when you have to move on. I was fortunate that when the time came for me to leave, Restore, a charity that provides homes for people leaving emergency housing had a place for me to go.

I've been with Restore two-and-a-half years now. There are four of us in a shared house. I've developed friendships, which is far more important to me than just providing a room and a roof. I see a mental health nurse twice a week and I get endless encouragement from the team at Restore which makes me feel incredibly safe and secure.

It hasn't been an overnight experience, but I believe that God, with people's help, has been working to change my outlook. I've been going to church regularly for a couple of years now and next month I get baptised. Of course, I know that just because you become a Christian doesn't mean that you're not going to have problems. I've still had some very serious times, but I've not let that push me back to where I was. I've carried on and made more progress. Today, I see a much more positive future than I did last year or the year before. I feel that there is a lot of opportunity for me to do something worthwhile in my life and at 45 years old I'm more confident about that than I was twenty years ago.

When I was younger my goals were all materialistic. I was working for a bigger house or a better car or a more exotic holiday. I'm not saying that it wouldn't be nice to visit new places, but I've lived without those things for so long that I don't think I need them anymore. I'm far more interested in people and building relationships, things we have for free and can so easily take for granted. I don't compare myself to other people anymore. I want to be a better person for myself. I'm a work in progress and, although there is a long way to go, I know I'm on the right path because now I can see a future and just the thought of that is exciting.

18 'God had other plans'

Tracey Ingram

'I know your works. Look, I have set before you an open door, which no one is able to shut. I know that you have but little power, and yet you have kept my word and have not denied my name' (Revelation 3:8).

John Sentamu writes:

Tracey's story of hope reminds us that the God who rescued us in Jesus Christ knows us and has plans for our future, and for our good. We may think we know the way we are going, but we may find that God is guiding us down some unexpected pathways – helping us to find *his* path, rather than the one we have carved out for ourselves.

Of course, knowing that God has a plan doesn't always make life easy! When we attempt to serve God, we often meet with obstacles and resistance; but when we are walking on the path prepared by God, things happen. Obstacles are removed, doors are opened, for *we are what he has made us, created in Christ Jesus for good works, which God prepared beforehand to be our way of life' (Ephesians 2:10)*.

In Tracey's story, we can sense that God has seen the path clearly and has prepared the way ahead for her. First, by giving her the gifts and talents, the love for people and the trust in God she needs, and then by gently directing her feet.

And as a Parish Nurse, Tracey is able to pray with her patients and help them, in turn, to walk on the path which their loving God has prepared for them, for their good.

✠

Tracey Ingram's story:

As a teenager adults would always ask me, 'What do you want to do when you leave school?' I never knew what to say. I wanted to work with people, but I never had a particular job in mind. One of my Girl Guide leaders, who was a nurse, tried to get me to be more specific. 'Have you ever thought about nursing?' she asked.

'No way,' I replied, 'I'd never be a nurse. I can't stand blood and gore.'

I said that, but when the time came to find a work experience placement I offered to volunteer in the outpatient department of the local hospital. My plan was to work in physiotherapy, a job where I imagined myself caring for people without any blood involved. God clearly had other plans for me, although when my exam results came through, it didn't feel like that. When I didn't get the grades needed to study physiotherapy, it felt like my whole world had collapsed and my life would be ruined because of it. It was with a heavy heart that I applied to train as an enrolled nurse, for no other reason than I had to do something and I didn't know what else to do. Can you imagine my disappointment when I was turned down for that place too, this time for the opposite reason – my grades were too high.

The course leader suggested that I apply for a university nursing course. In Hull, nursing as a university degree course was only in its second year and I still wasn't convinced that it was the job for me. 'I'm not interested in the theory,' I said, 'I'm a practical person, so if I'm going to do nursing, I want to do it practically.'

'Well, if that's how you feel you can have a place to do state registered nursing, but you can't have a place for an enrolled nurse,' the woman running the courses told me. 'It's entirely up to you, but I suggest you go to university.'

Again it was with reluctance that I opted for state registration, but with hindsight God had me in the right place because a few years later enrolled nurses weren't recognised and everyone in that role had to do a transfer course to become a registered nurse to keep working.

Surprisingly, once I started nursing, the blood and gore that had initially put me off the job didn't bother me at all. I can't explain why that was. It's not as if I was incredibly squeamish to begin with, because from being a small child I'd done first aid, it was all part of being in the guides and scouts. I think it was the idea of what I might be faced with more than the reality that frightened me. When I was younger, my picture of nursing was working in Accident and Emergency, and the thought of dealing with people who had been seriously injured in whatever way was overwhelming. As part of my training I did spend some time in the emergency department, and to my surprise I quite enjoyed it. I knew that it wasn't what I wanted long-term. However, my reasoning wasn't because I was put off by blood, as I'd originally thought; it was more to do with wanting to be in a role where I could see people more than once and build a relationship with them. Relationships at work were always important to me and I would get infuriated on ward rounds when staff would refer to a patient as the appendix in bed so and so. I'd say, 'That appendix is a person with a name. He is a human being who is ill, not a body part that needs fixing.'

In this respect my first job as a qualified nurse was ideal for me. I worked as part of the renal team looking after people who were receiving kidney dialysis treatment. I was dialysing people using bags of fluid rather than a machine, so my time was split between working at the hospital and in people's homes. I enjoyed working in the community because it enabled me to build relationships, not only with the person I was treating but with their family as well. If it wasn't for the unsociable hours, which I couldn't manage with a young family, I would probably still be in that job today.

When I was expecting my son I asked to reduce my hours but it wasn't possible. Despite being told, by people senior to me, that I was throwing my career away and I'd never get back into the job, I chose to stop work altogether and be a full-time mum for a while. During those next three years I came back to the faith I'd left behind as a teenager and began to recognise how God was working in my life, and usually this was when I couldn't see why things were going in the direction they were. When I did eventually come back to work I knew that God's hand was in it, because most people would say that there was no way I could walk away from my career for three years and come back into a community post – it was just unheard of. Although I couldn't say it was the perfect role, I knew that it was unusual for someone in my position to be considered for the job, and that I was fortunate to get it. I was working six hours a week as a Practice Nurse in a GP surgery. It didn't seem like much, but it was a foot in the door, and less than twelve months later when I applied to another GP surgery, I was offered a full time job as a Practice Nurse.

To encourage myself at work I pinned a picture on the wall of a kitten hanging onto a tree branch, with the words, 'I can hang on, Lord, as long as I know you're with me.' I'd put it there for me, but often other people would notice it and say to me, 'I'd really like prayer about this but I know you can't do that here. Will you add me to your prayer list?' The NHS is now moving towards more holistic care, but at the time it was difficult to respond to such requests. The patients understood my hesitation because there had been stories in the news about nurses who offered patients prayer and later found their jobs under threat.

I've never hidden my beliefs because I've always felt that you can't separate physical, mental and spiritual health. In my experience, very often you won't see any improvement in a person's physical health if their mental and spiritual health is not cared for too. My view is that practical and spiritual care are part of a holistic gospel message, but I didn't know how to achieve that vision at the time. The nearest I could get to it was at the ladies' Bible study group I facilitated at church. Each week before the group started someone would ask me a health related question because I was a nurse. Often I would sit down and have a coffee with people, listen to what was troubling them, and let them know in my professional opinion what help was available. If I had time, sometimes I would go along to hospital appointments with people for support and reassurance, or to make sure that they understood what was being said. One day, one of the ladies in the group said to me, 'You know, you should be our nurse. Well, when I say our nurse, I mean the church or parish nurse?'

'That's a nice thought,' I said laughing, 'but unfortunately that kind of job doesn't exist.'

I thought no more about it until a couple of years later when I picked up a magazine and read an article written by a Baptist minister, who was trying to bring parish nursing to the UK from the United States. In the article he talked about supporting people in prayer and offering health advice as part of life in the church. What he described was similar to what I was already doing with the lady's fellowship group. As I read on my stomach flipped, 'What are you trying to tell me here, Lord?' The words were recognition that jobs like the one I'd dreamed of did exist, and that there was potential for the role to be even more than I had imagined. I had to read it a couple of times just to take it in. I could hardly believe it was real. I'd being doing a lot of what the article described already, but not in any sort of structured way. Seeing it written down made me think about what I was doing in a different way.

In my excitement I handed the article to a project manager who was working on a building project at the church. 'Do you know much about parish nursing?' I asked. He didn't, but asked me to leave it with him and 24 hours later he came back to me.

'I've looked into parish nursing and we can get funding for this on the back of the project we've just done,' he said enthusiastically.

This was unexpected and brilliant news. The only trouble being, our parish vicar was on holiday for a couple of weeks and I didn't want to go any further with the idea without his agreement.

'We can still go ahead and apply for the funding,' the project manager said. 'If we get it, maybe it's a God thing, and if the vicar says, no, then we can always hand the money back and say it didn't work out.'

It felt like I was running before I could walk, but at the same time I felt that God had his hand on the idea somewhere, because within three weeks we'd applied for funding, been given a pot of money which included salary, and the vicar had returned from holiday and thought it was a fantastic idea. There was still the question of what to do about my job? I thought about being a parish nurse part-time, on my day off, but when I prayed about it the answer that always came back was, if I wanted to do this properly, then I needed to commit to it. I knew that was right because often my non-working day would be swapped around at short notice which made it difficult to plan other commitments around my work. That said, leaving my job was still a big decision, because the initial funding only lasted a year and at the time my husband and I were supporting our three children through university.

'Go for it,' my husband said, 'If God wants us to do it then he'll provide for us.'

That was five years ago, we took the leap of faith and since then parish nursing has grown beyond anything I could have imagined. I work with people of all ages and from all backgrounds, people who have different faiths and those who have none. If people don't want prayer that is fine, but the option is there. Parish nursing gives me the opportunity to offer whole person healthcare, allowing me to combine my profession with my faith, to carry out preventative healthcare together with spiritual care, enabling me to offer prayer alongside practical help and advice. It's not instead of the health service, it's an additional support that can help people access health services appropriately and understand their medication, care and condition. At St Aidan's I work with a team of volunteers and in addition to offering one-to-one support we run groups for walking, healthy eating, healthy cooking, keep fit and chair exercises, as well as more social groups like crafts and afternoon tea. One of the most rewarding parts of my job is seeing people, who might have been socially isolated, for whatever reason, start to get involved in the community again and in doing so, begin to help and support other people.

When I started out five years ago there were no parish nurses further north than the East Midlands. Now there are five of us within the Hull and Humber area alone. I don't know what will happen next but looking back it makes it easier for me to trust that God is going to look after me. People often ask, 'Where are you with your faith when things go wrong?' For me, that questioning doesn't come into it, because when I look back at my life I can see that God has guided me to the right path before so I know that he will do it again. When I find myself in the middle of a dark patch, although I may not be able to see where I'm going, I know that God is there and that he can see a way where I can't. I work with lots of people who have hit a rough patch in life and from my own experience I can tell them, keep your eyes focused and God will carry your hope for you. While you're in this dark patch, rely on us and rely on God, and know that, although I can't tell you how, you will come out the other side.

19 'I'm 59, and my life's just starting!'

Paul Myers

Then the son said to him, 'Father, I have sinned against heaven and before you; I am no longer worthy to be called your son.' But the father said to his slaves, 'Quickly, bring out a robe – the best one – and put it on him; put a ring on his finger and sandals on his feet. And get the fatted calf and kill it, and let us eat and celebrate; for this son of mine was dead and is alive again; he was lost and is found!' And they began to celebrate (Luke 15:21-24).

John Sentamu writes:

This passage comes from a well-known story commonly called 'The Parable of the Prodigal Son' – though Jesus spoke of 'a father who had two sons' and never used the words 'prodigal son'. The parable tells of a younger son who takes his future inheritance from his father, turns it into cash, and goes into a far country where he squanders all his liquid assets (cash) in living prodigally, extravagantly. Penniless and hungry he comes to his senses and decides to return home. This was not easy. It meant admitting mistakes and risking rejection – he had already received his inheritance and treated his father as though he were dead! He realised his situation was something that he deserved. He returned home to beg forgiveness and was overwhelmed by his father's enthusiastic welcome and loving embrace.

In a similar way, Paul shares his story of how he too he plunged into a lifestyle of music and alcohol dependency. He too, has had to face a moment of realisation. He had to choose to take the seemingly difficult path of admitting to past mistakes and of working towards a very different future. He later discovered the amazing power of love and forgiveness as he came home to God, looking to start again.

Paul's story shows how God's loving embrace is utterly transforming and illuminating. This time the party really can start!

Paul Myers' story:

The first time I saw The Beatles on TV I knew what I wanted to do with my life. I wanted to be a musician; but not just any musician, I wanted to be a drummer, I wanted to play like Ringo Starr. My parents didn't have the money to pay for music lessons, but I heard from a friend about free after-school tuition at Leeds Music Centre and went along. An old army drummer put a pair of sticks in my hand and a piece of music in front of me. I hit the drum skin and it felt amazing. It wasn't just a dream any more, I was playing the drums and I seemed to have an aptitude for it. Soon I was playing in the Yorkshire Schools' Brass Band and the Children's Youth

Symphony Orchestra. The enjoyment I got out of music was everything I'd always imagined and more.

At 16 I got my first opportunity to play with a big band. I turned to the bass player beside me and said: 'Wow, these guys can really play.'

He replied: 'Yes, and they can really drink as well.'

I soon learned that being a musician wasn't just about how well you could play, but how much you could drink and still play well. At that time, if I drank more than two halves I was giddy. I was working hard, I'd just started music college and was learning my craft, but I also wanted to stay in with these guys. They were real musicians – famous names. Being one of them made me successful, it was like a badge of honour.

The only drink I didn't touch was whisky, because I associated it with my father. My father was disappointed that I wanted to go to music college. He liked music but he couldn't see me making a living from it and advised me to get a proper job. Although it wasn't a trade, music was my job, and once I left college at 21 I never had a day out of work for 30 years.

I was different to my father, or so I thought. I drank Cognac. I liked the smooth taste and it sounded sophisticated. When I was still at music college a landlord said to me: 'Have you seen that lady at the end of the bar?'

'Yeah, what's she drinking?'

'Milk,' he said.

'Milk? In a pub? That's weird,' I said.

'That's because she used to drink what you're drinking.'

I dismissed the comment at the time, but 40 years later he was right, Cognac was to become my poison. The problem was, when I had a drink I was very much like my father. I was unpredictable and nasty. One minute I could be charming and the next I could say the most terribly abusive things, usually to people who loved me.

My father was a very troubled man and a binge drinker. Even though he worked in a munitions factory and my mother worked as a nurse, we were always struggling to put food on the table because every time we got some money my father would drink it. All my mates at school were wearing trendy clothes but my family could never afford to buy them for me. As an escape I threw myself into my music, and I made a decision that when I grew up I would have everything I wanted.

On my twenty-first birthday my father committed suicide. Before he took his life my father called me on the phone and told me what he was going to do. 'Good,' I said. I'd lived in fear for so long that I thought we'd all be better off without him. That's not how I feel now, but at the time there was a sense of relief, that the burden would be gone.

I didn't see any commonality between my drinking and my father's drinking. I enjoyed drinking and it was fun. I surrounded myself with like-minded people because I didn't want any criticism. I couldn't understand people who didn't drink. If you asked for a lemonade at the bar then you wouldn't be part of my gang. I was completely oblivious to the harm I was causing. I used to think because I didn't hit anybody that it was ok. I didn't realise that mental cruelty can be just as damaging to people and to personal relationships as a pair of fists can be.

It was expected that musicians would behave badly and it was surprising how quickly I began to make the same excuses. If I'd been nasty to someone I'd say, 'I'm really sorry, I was drunk,' as if that excused it all. I wasn't really sorry because I did it again and again, day in and day out.

When I was 24, I married but we divorced after a couple of years and I met a girl who was a singer. She liked a Bohemian lifestyle, she liked to party and she liked me. Not only was I attracted to her, but I thought that a musician and a singer seemed a great union. For a long time it was. We were married for 21 years and travelled the world together, working on luxury cruise liners.

When I started working on cruise ships I was introduced to more expensive tastes. My earning capacity was going up but I was ploughing it back into a grandiose lifestyle. I was a posh drunk, wearing a tuxedo and drinking martinis like James

Bond. I drank beer like everyone else, but I wouldn't drink any bottled beer, it had to be real ale. I developed a palate for the best quality wine, and there was always the Cognac.

My wife enjoyed a drink too, but she knew when to stop. I would keep drinking until I passed out. I'd wake up in the morning with no recollection of the night before. Then paranoia would set in about what I'd done, where I'd been, who I'd been with or what I'd said. I'd think, it'll be different next time. I'll only have a couple of drinks and I'll behave myself. After a couple of drinks I'd forget my resolve and the cycle would start again, until one night my wife said to me, 'I've had enough'.

I didn't understand what she was talking about at first. 'You've had enough of what?' I said.

'I've had enough of watching you drink yourself unconscious every night with a bottle of Cognac. I just can't take any more'.

We decided to split our assets and I decided to drink myself to death with the money. My father had died when he was 54, so in my head that was how long I would live. Until then I was going to spend all my money on having a great time.

If I was going to go out in a blaze of glory it would be good to have someone share it with and it wasn't long before I found her. I fell head over heels and we enjoyed the best of everything. I took her to Las Vegas, we stayed in the Bellagio, and she married me.

I loved to be extravagant and I thought that my wife would appreciate all the good restaurants and the fine wine, but after a few years she told me: 'You do that for you, Paul, none of that is for me. You like me to be in a restaurant not to spoil me, but so that I can be a witness to your drinking; someone to talk to'.

I didn't agree at the time, but when I look back she was right; it was all about me, all my relationships were about me and what I could get out of them. I knew she loved me and she tried to help me control my drinking. I went for support, but it was more to stop her nagging than because I wanted to. I was frightened to stop drinking, it was all I'd ever known and I didn't know what I would be like without it. At first I was asked to stop drinking for a day, which I did, then I went another day without a drink, and then another. I got a job and everything was going really well until one Friday I decided that I wanted a drink. Instead of going to my support meeting I drew £7000 out of the bank, booked into a hotel and went to the bar. I thought that I would stay there for a couple of days. Three weeks later I was still there, drinking night and day. That was the point at which my wife kicked me out.

I'd been dishonest with my wife; I hadn't told her about my plan to die. The breakdown of our marriage wasn't going to stop me. It wasn't long before everyone could see what I was doing and I was barred from every pub in town.

I couldn't understand it, I was a good customer. I'd buy everyone in the place a drink of whatever they wanted. I never caused any aggravation, I was the biggest spender in town. 'Why have you barred me?' I asked one of the managers.

'We won't be party to you destroying yourself, Paul.'

Fine, I thought, if he won't serve me, someone else will. So, I went into another bar. I had £2000 cash on me and I wanted to spend it.

'What are you doing here?' another manager asked me. 'You shouldn't be in here.'

The next thing I knew, the police arrived and took me to my estranged wife's house.

'We've had a call that he's very vulnerable. We found him in a bar waving a lot of money around,' the policeman said.

'He doesn't live here,' said my wife, 'but I'll take him tonight.'

Looking back, there were lots of people helping me, I just couldn't see it. I was on a path of self-destruction and I wasn't going to be deterred. I had a flat in town but when I left my wife's home the next day, I booked into a hotel. It was part of the grandiose way in which I wanted to end it all. I'd taken to drinking first thing in the morning and would get the shakes if I didn't have any alcohol, I needed it so desperately.

Early one Sunday I was walking through the city when I caught sight of my reflection in a glass window. 'Who's that?' I thought, then I realised the person looking back at me, was me. It was pouring with rain and I was shaking because I needed a drink, but my shock at seeing my reflection was about more than how terrible I looked physically. I didn't recognise who I was inside either. I looked completely lost and utterly broken, as though I had lost every sense of hope and purpose in my life. All I wanted was a drink, despite all the evidence that it wasn't good for me. At that point I realised something had to change. A couple of days of oblivion followed. I took an overdose and thought that would be it, but it wasn't, I was still here. I'd racked up so much debt that I wondered if I could go to prison. I wouldn't be able to drink in prison. It was an insane thought, and then I had another – I'll have one last weekend in Leeds to say goodbye to drinking.

I don't know what I expected the weekend to bring, but it was uneventful in the sense that, for me, drinking until I passed out wasn't anything unusual. The following Monday morning I went to a bar and ordered a drink. I started drinking, but it wasn't what I wanted. If I was going to change then I had to start there and then.

I left my glass half full on the bar and walked to the train station. The next trains to depart were going to London and York. I sat staring at the notice-board. London or York? If I go to London I'll drink myself to death, I thought. If I go to York I might have a chance.

In my head moving to York symbolised a new start. I didn't stop drinking straight away but I did seek out help and, this time, I was ready for it. All I wanted was some peace, to find a bit of calm in the chaos. I started searching spiritually. In the past I wanted to be king of my own life. Now I'd lost everything it seemed like a good idea to get to know God. I prayed for help every day, taking one day at a time. Six months later, I realised that I didn't think about drinking any more. The realisation was so overwhelming that I didn't dare to think about it. All I knew was that I hadn't changed on my own.

If God could do that for me, what else could he do? The answer was more than I could have ever believed possible. He's reconciled all my relationships and brought me to new ones. I wrote to my wife of 21 years and asked if she'd meet me, so I could apologise for the way I behaved during our marriage. I wasn't sure what to expect, but she called me the following day and agreed to meet me. After we divorced she remarried and moved to Scotland. We met for a coffee in Edinburgh and her husband came with her. I started to take accountability for what I'd done and she stopped me. 'It's ok, Paul, I forgive you,' she said. It turns out that she had come to faith about the same time as me. Now we meet regularly and we pray together.

I'm also on good terms with my third wife and she is amazed at the changes in me. I'm not carrying as much pain as I used to. After my father committed suicide I carried around so much hurt and unforgiveness about it. I tried to let it go, but I couldn't. Once I began praying my heart changed – I was able to forgive my father. It's been an incredible journey.

It's four years since God removed the desire for me to drink alcohol and all sense of me wanting to destroy myself. I'm 59 and it feels like my life is only just starting, it's awesome.

20 'Supported by other people's prayers'

Marilyn Marshall

'Are any among you sick? They should call for the elders of the church and have them pray over them, anointing them with oil in the name of the Lord' (James 5:14).

John Sentamu writes:

In reading Marilyn's story of hope, we come to understand what it means to be carried on the prayers of others.

Prayer is a profound mystery. In bringing people to God in prayer we have no idea or forewarning of what God might do; but we are invited to come to him and to trust him.

Friends, prayer is not like a slot machine, where you can pull the lever and the desired object magically appears! We pray because in doing so, we are sharing in God's continual work of love and care. He is there before us in every situation, and we are invited to join in what he is doing.

Yes, prayer at times may seem like shouting into a concrete bucket, and we can't always understand why some people get well when we pray and others don't. But, as we find in Marilyn's story, when we pray for healing, God meets us in the midst of our deepest need; he lifts us up, and takes away our fear.

Marilyn Marshall's story:

I've worked in the ambulance service for 25 years, so I'm used to being in a hospital every day and seeing how many people, young and old, use the services. For much of that time I was a driver, picking people up from their homes and taking them to hospital for cancer treatment. Usually treatment would be booked in blocks, once a day for 15 sessions, so I'd meet the same people on a regular basis. I'd ask how they were doing and try to encourage them. 'They have great treatment these days ...You've got to go through this and then you'll be fine ... I know Mrs So-and-So, who had the same as you, and she's fine now.' I'd say those things because I believed them. I wanted to help people and I wanted them to get better. If I'd spoken like that to people so many times and didn't apply those same words to myself, did I really believe them to be true?

I was diagnosed with breast cancer after a routine mammogram. The news came as a shock because I had no symptoms, none that I was aware of anyway. It was my turn to be the patient now. All those positive things I'd said to people over the years, I had to apply them to myself. If I'd believed those things for other people, why couldn't I believe them for myself? The truth was, although I always came across as a jolly person who could laugh things off easily, inside I'd often feel horrible. I often spoke negatively to myself and it wasn't easy to think in a different way. So, while my first instinct was to think, this treatment isn't going to work, I had to keep telling myself, this treatment is going to work, I am going to get over this, and I will be well again.

I had a lumpectomy followed by radiotherapy treatment. Tests on my lymph glands didn't show any sign of cancer, so I was told that I didn't need any chemotherapy. My son's girlfriend had breast cancer when she was 30 years old. I felt that I could ask her anything and she wouldn't think it was daft, because she'd been through the same things, and she understood. She made sure that I looked after myself properly and would chop all kinds of different fruit and vegetables and blend them into smoothie drinks that she said were full of vitamins. They looked ghastly, but she said that they were good for me so I gave them a try and after a while they didn't taste so bad. She was a real support for me in that way, and in keeping me upbeat too.

After five years I was given the all clear from the hospital. Everything was fine, until early the following year. I felt exhausted, but I'd been so busy over the Christmas period that I thought I'd just over done it. Then I started with a pain that got worse. I ended up going to casualty where I was admitted to hospital. When I was first examined the doctors thought that I had gall stones, but further tests revealed that I was suffering due to secondary liver cancer, caused by cells from the breast cancer that had been dormant for six years.

My first thoughts were that I'd had a raw deal, that if I'd had chemotherapy all those years ago it would have killed those cells in the beginning so they couldn't have spread. Perhaps it would or perhaps it wouldn't. All I knew was that I was having to go through the same investigations and uncertainty all over again and I wasn't sure I could cope. Before long I became very ill with complications which meant that I was in and out of hospital on a regular basis.

The high levels of bilirubin in my liver made me jaundiced. I'd say to my husband, Rod, 'Do I look really yellow today?'

'No,' he'd say.

I'd look in the mirror and think, 'Yes, I do'.

I looked awful, but Rod never told me that. He is always so positive, which is why I couldn't understand it when he contacted our youngest son and his girlfriend who were travelling in Australia and asked them to come home. I was annoyed at Rod for cutting their trip short because I didn't realise how poorly I was.

My son and his girlfriend are the type of couple who are simply meant to be together. In their minds they didn't need to be married because they were never going to be apart, but they knew that their wedding was something I'd like to see. So, they got a special license to be married quickly. When the time came my condition had deteriorated further. I was too weak to take even a mild form of chemotherapy and found myself in a hospice being told that I had only two weeks to live.

During that time I received more than 250 cards from well-wishers and every day had someone visit me. It didn't register at the time how much I was being carried by other people. It wasn't that I was unappreciative; I was so unwell that I couldn't be bothered with anything. There were no mirrors in the hospice, so I didn't even know what I looked like anymore, but to be honest I couldn't have cared.

Although I had no energy for most things, I did still want to see my son get married. When that day arrived my friend came into the hospice to help me get ready. I had to use oxygen for most of the day, but she helped me to wash and style my hair and to get dressed. When I finally saw myself in the mirror it felt like I'd been transformed. 'Oh, that's me,' I said. 'I look like my old self again.' I got a real boost from that thought, and I found the strength to leave my wheelchair and walk the short distance up the aisle to give the bride away. His girlfriend had been such a support to me through my illness that I wanted to do this for her. It was the most wonderful occasion, I couldn't stop smiling.

I think that day signalled one of many turning points for me. I realised that I had life in me yet, and after two weeks in the hospice, my liver results showed a slight improvement, enough that a consultant suggested I could try some chemotherapy tablets and see what happened.

I decided to give the medication a whirl and Rod organised facilities in our house so that I could be looked after at home. My husband is a vicar, and shortly after I came home the Archbishop of York, John Sentamu, visited the Romero Project attached to Rod's parish. As part of the visit, Rod had arranged for the Archbishop to come to see me. I wish Rod had told me about it, because I looked an absolute state when the Archbishop arrived. On reflection, it was probably best that he hadn't, because I only would have worried about it, and there was no need. The Archbishop was so easy to talk to, and just his presence in the room gave me a lift. I can't remember exactly how he put it, but as he anointed me, the Archbishop said something like: 'We need people like you, Marilyn. You're not going anywhere'. Once he told me that, I began to start believing it too.

My recovery felt slow at times, but my health was picking up. I started moving a little more every day until I could walk to the garden gate and back. Later I would walk to the church at the end of the road. Every year we take a parish trip to the shrine of Our Lady of Walsingham. It's a very special place for me. That year I needed a wheelchair to get around but I was overwhelmed to think that I'd managed to get there. When I looked around me I realised how much I'd been supported by other people's prayers – that I wasn't on my own. To think that other people had taken time to include me in their prayers was amazing. It made me think more deeply about my own prayers and how I could widen them to include other people, not just those I knew needed help, but people I had seen or heard about on the news.

I'd always been the kind of person who needed to know what to do in a situation. When I prayed, I always thought I'd like God to give me a straight answer or at least reveal a drop-down box that gave me a set of choices. When I was very ill, I couldn't do anything – I didn't even have the strength to pray.

Some of the time I was hallucinating and I'm not sure that anything I said made much sense. As time went on I learned that there were some things I had to let be. I had to trust. It was as if I had to put into practice what I'd always been taught, and place my life in God's hands.

Being in Walsingham was an emotional weekend. I shed a lot of tears, but at the same time, I felt as if I was learning to let go of some of the pain – to leave my heartache in Walsingham rather than carrying it with me all the time. It was like someone had taken a huge weight off my shoulders. I realised that I can't do it all on my own, but neither do I have to.

My eldest son and his wife were expecting their first child. None of us expected me to live to see the baby, so my son had a 4D scan taken to let me see the baby more clearly in the womb. I kept that photo in a frame and kept telling myself, 'I'm going to see this little girl'. I'd come through so much already, surely I could manage this one last thing.

My granddaughter is two-and-a-half-years-old now, and is the light of my life. After she was born, I could feel my strength growing and began to think about other things in my life again. My boss had visited me several times during my illness so I asked him, 'How would you feel about me coming back to work?'

I'd worked at the same place for many years, but I wasn't sure how he'd take my request. To my surprise he didn't even need to think about it. 'That's fine by me,' he said.

'You do know that I'll be classed as disabled' I said.

'Yes. We'll work with you to get back to work if that's what you want.'

I've been back at work for two years now. I'm in a different role, because I can't be out on the road in the same way, but it's brought a bit of normality back into my life. I still have hospital appointments every three weeks. I take chemotherapy tablets for two weeks and then have a week off. Last week my liver function results came back normal. I don't think the cancer has gone away completely, but it has been contained and I don't worry about it now in the same way. Like Rod says to me, 'You can be in the waiting room for next life, but we're all terminally ill if you think about it. We're all going to die one day, it's just a question of when. I could walk across that road outside the church and be run over by a bus.'

Rod is right. Just because I have cancer doesn't mean my life has ended. I only have to look at my dad to see that. He celebrated his ninetieth birthday last week, and has had prostate cancer for at least 25 years. Of course, it could have been very different, but we never know what life will bring. I know that I have changed because of my experience. I used to worry a lot more and was always very cautious. Living that way can stop you enjoying life. Now, I'll treat myself. I'm not silly with money, but I will enjoy it. If Rod and I go somewhere special, we'll buy a nice lunch out and I won't begrudge it. It's a treat for us that makes for a memorable day and when I look back, that's what I'll remember – that we were together, it was special time, and we had a lovely day.

DARTON·LONGMAN + TODD

Darton, Longman and Todd is as an internationally-respected publisher of brave, ground-breaking and independent books on matters of heart, mind and soul that meet the needs and interests of ordinary people.

Our books are written by, and for, people of all faiths and none. We believe that spirituality and faith are important to all people, of all backgrounds, and that the wisdom of any one culture or tradition can inform and nourish another.

We also publish the Jerusalem Bible, and its revised and updated successor, the New Jerusalem Bible – one of the most clear, accurate and distinguished modern English translations of the Bible.

For more information on DLT, and to buy our books, please visit our website
www.dltbooks.com
or visit your local bookshop. You can stay up to date with our activities by following us on Twitter @dlt_books

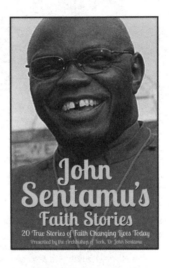

DΛRTON·LON6MAN+TODD

INCLUSIVE CHURCH

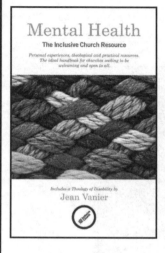

Mental Health	Disability
The Inclusive Church Resource	The Inclusive Church Resource
Personal experiences, theological and practical resources. The ideal handbook for churches seeking to be welcoming and open to all.	*Personal experiences, theological and practical resources. The ideal handbook for churches seeking to be welcoming and open to all.*
Includes a Theology of Disability by Jean Vanier	*Includes a Theology of Disability by* John M Hull

978-0-232-52966-7	978-0-232-53065-0
£8.99	£8.99

There is a huge need for churches to be more inclusive – some might be more inclusive in some areas than others (both in attitude and resources), but on the whole this is a massive failing of churches. Most church leaders recognise this failing but lack the resources and understanding to effect meaningful change. The Inclusive Church Resources aim to educate, to reflect theologically and to provide practical advice and guidance.

The General Editor of each book is **Bob Callaghan**, national co-ordinator of Inclusive Church, a cross-denominational organisation committed to working for a church that is welcoming and open to all. Authors include **Jean Vanier** and **John M Hull**.

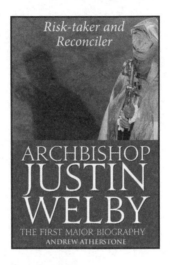